THE RESURRECTION OF CHRIST

THE RESURRECTION
OF CHRIST

AN EXAMINATION OF THE APOSTOLIC BELIEF
AND ITS
SIGNIFICANCE FOR THE CHRISTIAN FAITH

BY THE REV.

JOHN MACKINTOSH SHAW, M.A.(Edin.)

PROFESSOR OF APOLOGETICS AND SYSTEMATIC THEOLOGY IN THE
PRESBYTERIAN COLLEGE, HALIFAX, NOVA SCOTIA

EDINBURGH: T. & T. CLARK, 38 GEORGE STREET
1920

TO

MY MOTHER

PREFACE

THIS work is the outcome of requests made to the Publishers from different quarters for the publication in separate book form of the Article on the "Resurrection of Christ" in the recently issued second volume of Hastings' *Dictionary of the Apostolic Church*.

The opportunity has been taken to expand and amplify the original Article at different points with a view to greater clearness and explicitness of position. Especially is this the case with the chapters dealing with the nature of our Lord's Resurrection-Body. It is the writer's conviction that the "reduced" or "attenuated" Christianity which is the outcome of indifference to the bodily aspect of the Resurrection not only does less than justice to Apostolic thought, but has serious consequences for our belief in the centrally determinative and constitutive significance of the Resurrection of Christ for our view of the world and life, and in particular for our belief in the ultimate subjugation of the entire material order to the purposes of spirit. In this expanded and amplified form the writer hopes that the book has become a little more worthy of the exceedingly generous reception given the original Article in British and American reviews.

The Author's thanks are due to his colleague, Professor J. W. Falconer, D.D., for his kindness in reading the proofs and making helpful suggestions.

PRESBYTERIAN COLLEGE, HALIFAX, N.S.,
May 1920.

CONTENTS

THE
RESURRECTION OF CHRIST

CHAPTER I

THE PLACE OF THE RESURRECTION OF CHRIST IN THE APOSTOLIC CHURCH

THE fundamental fact on which the Apostolic Church rests is the resurrection of Jesus Christ. What lies at the basis of everything else, determining the whole round of apostolic thought and life, is the conviction that the Jesus who was crucified was raised from the grave by the power of God and is now the Exalted and Sovereign Lord. Apart from this the very existence of Apostolic Christianity as exhibited in the New Testament is unintelligible and inexplicable. Three aspects of this fundamental significance of the Resurrection may here be indicated.

(a) It is the fontal source or spring of the apostolic faith, that which brought the Church into existence, and set it moving with that wonderful vitality and power which lie before us in the New Testament.

Much of modern historical criticism attempts to find the impulse which constitutes Christianity in the impression of the life and teaching of Jesus on His disciples. But so far as that went, and if that were all, there would have been no such thing as the Christianity of the apostles. There might have been memoirs of Him, there might have been a school of thought founded on His teaching, but there would have been no living faith, no Christian gospel, no Apostolic Church. He had spoken as no man had ever spoken; He had done many mighty works, "works which none other man did" (John xv. 24). And more than what He said and did was what He was—the unique impression of His life and personality, whereby He made men feel that in Him they were face to face with one who was none other than the great Promised One of God, "the Christ" (Mark viii. 29; Matt. xvi. 16; Luke ix. 20), "the Holy One of God" (John vi. 69; cf. Acts iii. 14, "the Holy and Righteous One"). Yet the faith called forth by the life of Christ was a faith which broke into fragments under the crash of the Cross. The creative force or dynamic of Christianity has, as a matter of history, to be found in an event that carries us beyond the limits of the earthly life. It was the Resurrection, viewed as a great declaratory act of God, the fact that God "raised him from the dead, and made him to sit at his right hand" (Eph. i. 20), that re-interpreted and re-established the faith evoked by the Life, and for the first time gave Him His true place as Lord and Christ in their lives.

This is best seen by reference to the reports of St. Peter's speeches in the Acts, in which, by general consent, we have a true representation of the earliest Christian preaching. In these speeches St. Peter starts indeed from the historical Person of Jesus and from facts well known to his hearers regarding His life on earth : " Jesus of Nazareth, a man accredited to you by God through miracles and wonders and signs which God performed by him among you, as you yourselves know " (Acts ii. 22) ; " anointed with the Holy Ghost and with power : who went about doing good, and healing all that were oppressed of the devil ; for God was with him " (x. 38). This Divine approval of Jesus on earth, as certified by His works, was, however, apparently contradicted and denied by His death on the Cross, which to the Jew was the symbol of Divine rejection (v. 30, x. 39 ; cf. Deut. xxi. 23). But the difficulty thus presented to faith by His death was removed or annulled by the Resurrection on " the third day " (x. 40), which is represented as a great historical act on the part of God, Who thereby reversed Israel's act of rejection and vindicated the claim of Jesus to be the Christ, " whom ye crucified, whom God raised " (iv. 10 ; cf. ii. 24, 32, 36, iii. 15). Thus through the Resurrection Jesus is proclaimed not only as " Messiah " (iii. 18–20, iv. 25–28), but as " Lord " (i. 21, ii. 21, 33, 36, iii. 13, 21, v. 31, x. 36), " Saviour " (v. 31 ; iv. 12, " In none other is there salvation "), " Prince of life " (iii. 15, v. 31), and " Judge of quick and dead " (x. 42, represented as in accordance with the teaching of Jesus Himself). So men are called to repentance and to be baptized in the name of Christ for the remission of sins and receiving of the gift of the Holy Spirit (ii. 38, x. 43).

(b) Not only is the resurrection of Christ the fontal source or spring of Apostolic Christianity, so that from it the apostolic gospel dates ; it is itself the very centre and substance of this gospel.

So far from being a mere accessary or appendage to the apostolic message, a detached event added on to the life and teaching of Jesus to assure the disciples of His survival of death and of the truth of His claim, in it lay germinally and as in a kernel the whole gospel they had to preach ; so that the preaching of Christ is for the apostles the preaching of His resurrection, and their primary function is to be witnesses of the fact (Acts i. 8, 22, etc.).   St. Paul but represented the common apostolic mind when, writing to the Corinthians, he said : "If Christ hath not been raised, then is our preaching vain " (κενόν, there is nothing in it, it has no real content), and "your faith is vain (ματαία, it is futile, to no purpose, fruitless of effect) ; ye are yet in your sins" (1 Cor. xv. 14, 17).   If Christ died and in that "lorn Syrian town" lies in His grave like other men, then the whole gospel of the apostles falls to the ground, for the good news they have to declare is that God hath raised up Jesus from the dead and made Him the Exalted Lord to whom all power is given in heaven and on earth. "This Jesus whom ye crucified God hath made both Lord and Christ " (Acts ii. 36)—this is the concentrated essence of the gospel they proclaim.   There is nothing else in it except what comes out of this, and belongs to this, and is illumined by this.

It is the resurrection of Christ, viewed not as a mere revivification of His earthly body but as His entrance on a state of exalted power and Lordship, that provides the key which unlocks the inner meaning and significance of His earthly life and ministry.   In the light of it the earthly life of Jesus, with its amazing memories, is seen to be a very incarnation of God, a "sending forth" of His Son by the Father, the event to which all else in the world's history had been moving (Gal. iv. 4).   In the light of the Resurrection, too, the Death on the Cross, the very symbol of shame, which had seemed to wipe out for the disciples the meaning of the Life, becomes full of Divine meaning and significance, the central disclosure of redeeming self-sacrificing Love.

But more than this; the revelation of the life and death of Christ attained its end and became an effective reality only through the Resurrection.   For only through His being raised from the dead and His exaltation to supreme power and sovereignty with the redeeming virtue of His life and death in Him, did Christ enter fully on His career as Prince and Saviour (Acts v. 31), and become the life-giving principle of a new humanity (1 Cor. xv. 22), the second Adam (Rom. v. 12 f.; 1 Cor. xv. 45), inaugurating a new era in the process of Divine creative evolution.   The religion of the apostles is communion with a Risen Lord.   Only "in Him," "in Christ," in union with a living Saviour, have we redemption and renewal of life (e.g. Eph. i. 7; Col. i. 14, ii. 13; Rom. iii. 24).

(c) As the entrance of the crucified and buried Jesus on a state of exalted power and glory in which He is Lord both in grace and in nature, the Resurrection is, further, the fundamental determinative principle of the whole apostolic view of the world and life.   It pervaded and revolutionized their whole universe of thought, controlling and governing their interpretation of existence and creating a new intellectual perspective so that all things—God, the world, man—came to be viewed *sub specie Resurrectionis.*

The characteristic apostolic title for God becomes " God the Father who raised Jesus Christ from the dead " (*e.g.* Rom. iv. 24, vi. 4, viii. 11 ; Col. ii. 12 ; 1 Pet. i. 21). The God in whom they believe is One whose character is once for all made manifest in that He raised up Jesus Christ.   The Cross and the Burial had seemed to be the triumph of evil in the world, the final defeat of holy love.   But by the Resurrection and Exaltation God had vindicated the holiness of Jesus, and by thus vindicating Jesus had vindicated and authenticated Himself.   At the great crucial moment in the world's moral history, in the case of a perfectly holy life, the omnipotence of God — in apostolic language the " working of the strength of his might " (Eph. i. 19)—was shown to be on the side of goodness and righteousness.

Through the resurrection of Christ, too, as no merely spiritual resurrection—" the survival of the spirit beyond death "—but a being raised from the grave and from the power of death, God has convincingly manifested the supremacy of spirit over the strongest material forces.   The long struggle between nature and spirit was concentrated climactically in the body of Jesus, and by His bodily resurrection from death and the grave—and what other kind of resurrection from the grave could there be ?—victory is shown to remain with spirit. Death itself, the crowning manifestation of the seeming victory of material forces over spirit, has been vanquished and overcome; and this supreme and crucial revelation of the power and character of God sheds its transfiguring light over all other revelation in nature and history, illuminating the mysteries of life here and of destiny hereafter. By the Resurrection the final pledge and assurance of personal immortality is given to men; the present life in the fullness of its embodied existence is lifted above the vicissitudes of time and invested with infinite meaning and eternal value. " Wherefore "—such is the conclusion of St. Paul's great argument in the Resurrection chapter in 1 Cor.—" be ye stedfast, unmoveable, always abounding in the work of the Lord, forasmuch as ye know that your labour is not in vain in the Lord " (xv. 58). In a word, the resurrection of Christ was for the apostolic mind the one fact in which the world and history arrived at unity, consistency, coherence; the pledge and the guarantee of " the gathering together in one of all things in Christ " (Eph. i. 10; cf. Col. i. 15 ff.). It was the breaking in upon human life of a new world of triumph and hope, in which were contained at once the pledge and the ground of the consummation of God's purpose for the world. Hence the vitalizing and energizing optimism of the apostolic outlook on life—" born anew to a living hope through the resurrection of Jesus Christ from the dead " (1 Pet. i. 3).

That the Resurrection holds this place of centrally determinative importance in the Apostolic Church is a fact which, if not always sufficiently realized by the friends of Christianity in subsequent centuries, is at all events acknowledged by her opponents. D. F. Strauss, *e.g.*, the most trenchant and remorseless of her critics, in dealing with the Resurrection acknowledges that it is the " touch-stone not of lives of Jesus only, but of Christianity itself," that it " touches all Christianity to the quick," and is " decisive for the whole view of Christianity " (*New Life of Jesus*, Eng. tr., 2 vols., London, 1865, i. 41, 397). And P. W. Schmiedel, after recalling the cardinal Pauline doctrines as determined by his belief in the Resurrection, says : " It seems accordingly in logic inevitable that if at any time it should come to be recognized that the resurrection of Jesus never happened, the Christian faith with respect to all the points just mentioned would necessarily come to an end " (*Encycl. Biblica*, iv. 4039). If this goes, all that is vital and essential in Christianity goes ; if this remains, all else remains. So it is that through the centuries, from Celsus onwards, the Resurrection has been the storm centre of the attack upon the Christian faith.

The character of this attack has varied from age to age. To-day it differs in important respects from what it was even fifteen or twenty years ago. The application of new and more stringent methods of criticism to the evidence, the rich store of new material provided through recent researches in comparative religion and mythology, the re-discovery of Judaistic apocalyptic literature, and the new interest in the psychology of religion—all this has given " a new face " to the critical attack. It is not, indeed, that the apostolic belief in the resurrection of Christ, or the centrality of this belief to Apostolic Christianity, is denied. These are admitted on all sides as incontestable. What is called in question

is the validity of the belief, the historical reality of the
fact or facts on which the belief was based. It is held
that in the light of the new critical methods applied to
the evidence and the new knowledge made accessible to
us to-day, in the light of what is generally, though
ambiguously, called "modern thought," it is no longer
possible for us to believe in the Resurrection as the
apostles believed in it.   In particular, in much present-
day discussion it is maintained that, in view of modern
scientific-historical criticism of the evidence, it is impossible to believe in the resurrection of Christ in any other
sense than that of a spiritual resurrection.   The result
is that to-day we are faced with this somewhat new
situation, that not by the opponents of Christianity only
but by some of its most honoured supporters and
advocates, in their effort to recommend Christianity to
the "modern mind," the bodily resurrection of Christ is
denied or minimized as forming no vital or essential part
of the Christian faith.

In our treatment of the subject we shall first of
all examine the nature and extent of the historical
evidence which is presented in the apostolic writings
for the fact of the Resurrection, and thence educe the
nature or character of the apostolic belief in the fact.
Thereafter we shall consider the meaning or significance
of the Resurrection for Apostolic Christianity,—this in
itself is part of the apostolic evidence for the fact, as
the true nature of a cause becomes apparent only in
its effects,—and finally examine the main critical attempts
to explain the belief without acknowledging the fact.
In the course of the inquiry the conviction will be

expressed and supported that the recorded evidence for the resurrection of Christ, though in many ways disappointingly meagre and when critically examined not devoid of " contradictions," or " discrepancies," is yet adequate and sufficient for the purpose in view, and that those critics who come to negative conclusions do so less because of difficulties connected with the evidence than because of presuppositions or *præjudicia* of a dogmatic or philosophical character with which they come to the examination of the subject. The evidence available for the resurrection of Christ, it is recognized, can appeal aright only to those to whom the fact has a significance altogether different from that which an ordinary fact of human history can ever possess. Mere historical evidence is of itself incompetent to generate true Christian faith in the Resurrection. This depends on anterior and prior considerations determining our religious attitude to the fact—upon our philosophy of life and, in the last resort, upon our estimate of Jesus Christ Himself.

CHAPTER II

THE APOSTOLIC EVIDENCE FOR THE FACT OF THE RESURRECTION

I. THE PRIMARY EVIDENCE

IN proceeding to examine the evidence for the fact of the Resurrection, it should be remarked, to begin with, that this is much wider than is often represented. The direct historical evidence presented in the New Testament narratives of the empty grave on "the third day" and the self-manifestations of the Risen Lord—upon the examination of which the truth of the Resurrection is often decided—is after all but a part of the witness by which the fact is established. The primary evidence lies further back, in the transformation effected in the thoughts and lives of the apostles, giving rise to the Christian Church in the fullness of that energizing life and power of which the New Testament writings are themselves but the product.

To realize the greatness of this transformation we have but to take the picture of the apostles after the event as given in the Acts, and compare it with that before as given in the Gospels. Sadness has given place to joy, weakness to strength, cowardice to courage, despair to confidence. The men who, timorous and un-understanding, had forsaken their Master in His hour of utmost need, who counted all their hopes in Him lost when He was put to death, who, disillusioned and hopeless, had for fear of the Jews shut themselves up within closed doors, now face the rulers of the land proclaiming that He whom they had condemned and crucified was indeed the Christ, the Messiah, in whom alone there was salvation (Acts iv. 12), and summoning them to repentance and to baptism in His name for the remission of their sins and the receiving of the gift of the Holy Ghost (ii. 38).

Such a change, such a moral and spiritual transformation, with the results following, more detailed examination of which will be made later (Chap. VII.), demands a sufficient cause. What the apostles' own explanation was we know—the Resurrection "whereof we are witnesses" (Acts ii. 32, iii. 15, v. 32, x. 39, etc.). They believed that the Crucified Jesus was now the Risen and Exalted Lord, raised from the dead on the third day by the power of the Father—a belief which early found institutional expression in the observance of the first day of the week as "the Lord's Day." Whether they were deceived or not, is not now the question. It is sufficient at present to note that this is the fundamental or foundational evidence in relation to which all other evidence must be seen. "It is not this or that in the New Testament—it is not the story of the empty tomb, or of the appearing of Jesus in Jerusalem or in Galilee—which is the primary evidence for the resurrection ; it is . . . the existence of the Church in that extraordinary spiritual vitality which confronts us in the New Testament" (Denney, *Jesus and the Gospel*, p. 111 f.).

This is where the apostles themselves placed the emphasis. "He hath poured forth this which ye both see and hear" (Acts ii. 23), says St. Peter in his first sermon, referring to the gift of the Spirit at Pentecost as proof of the resurrection and exaltation of Christ; and in his second sermon or address the healing of the cripple is adduced as further proof (iii. 16). In his view the evidence of the Resurrection was not merely a past event "on the third day," with Appearings following, but that issuing in and attested by present religious experience. "The Resurrection was not an isolated event. . . . It was the beginning of a new and living relation between the Lord and His people. . . . The idea may be expressed by saying that the apostolic conception of the Resurrection is rather 'the Lord lives' than 'the Lord was raised' . . . Christ lives, for He works still" (Westcott, *The Gospel of the Resurrection*, p. 294 f.). Thus it is that the continued existence of the Church, and of the moral miracle in which the Church consists, is a vital part of the evidence for the Resurrection. "Deny the records; . . . but you are met by the advancing wave and that is no deception! Deny the Gospels; but the history itself confronts us; is its own evidence; tells its own story of something supernatural. . . . Something happened over eighteen centuries ago in Judæa, on the morning of the third day, which has changed the whole current and flow of history;—men's lives, their homes, the rights of children, the lot of slaves, the position of woman, the

whole order of society, all things human are taken up
into and swept along by a new resistless movement
which still bears upon the crest of its advancing wave
the hope of the world's future" (Newman Smyth,
Old Faiths in New Light, p. 155 f.). If the Resurrection
were not a fact thus continued into the present, the
historical incidents recorded would soon have faded, like
all merely historical facts, into a past significance.

The remembrance of this primary evidence for the Resurrection
has important consequences. (1) The Apostolic Church, the
Christian society, existed before any of the New Testament
narratives were written, and essentially is independent of them.
Therefore even if the narratives were, as alleged, "conflicting and
confused"—nay, even if it could be shown that there are features
in them whose historical value is doubtful, this would not of itself
disprove the fact of the Resurrection. We should in that case
know less than we thought we did about the mode of the Resurrection life of Christ, but our faith in the Resurrection itself, of which
the existence of the Church is the primary evidence, would not
necessarily be disturbed. (2) It is only in relation to this primary
evidence that the " historical evidence " presented in the narratives
can be estimated aright. The narratives were written from within
the Church, they were the product of the faith created by the
Resurrection. Further, they relate to a fact which is no mere event
of the past but continues as a living power in the present, and so
must be viewed in the context of living history and experience.
Historical criticism, therefore, which isolates the narratives from
this living context, and analyzes them out of relation on the one
hand to the experience of which they are the outcome, and on the
other to the experience in which they result, is in its nature
abstract, and can give only a limited or partial view of the facts.

CHAPTER III

THE APOSTOLIC EVIDENCE FOR THE FACT
OF THE RESURRECTION (*Continued*)

II. THE DOCUMENTARY EVIDENCE

WITH the fundamental and primary evidence for the Resurrection referred to before us, we pass to examine what is commonly called "the historical evidence," that presented in the New Testament documents or narratives.

1. THE WITNESS OF ST. PAUL

The earliest documentary evidence to the fact of the resurrection of Christ is that presented in the writings of St. Paul, and embraces two facts, the empty grave and subsequent appearings of the Risen Lord.

(a) *The Empty Grave*

St. Paul is sometimes appealed to in support of a purely spiritual Resurrection, as teaching that it was the spirit of Christ which rose into new life, and his view is contrasted with the "more materialized" representation of the Gospels. The empty grave and the resurrection of the Body were, it is alleged, no part of St. Paul's teaching, but a later development. Schmiedel, *e.g.*, supports his contention of the unhistorical character of the evidence for the empty tomb by reference to "the silence of Paul . . . a silence which would be wholly inexplicable were the story true" (*Encycl. Biblica*, iv. 4066). Weizsäcker urges that St. Paul says nothing of what happened at the grave because he knew nothing of it (*Apost. Age*[2], London, 1897–99, i. 5). And Harnack, while thinking it "probable" that the Apostle knew of the message about the empty grave, holds that "we cannot be quite certain about it." In any case, "certain it is that what he and the disciples regarded as all-important was not the state in which the grave was found, but Christ's appearances" (*What is Christianity?*, Eng. tr.[3], London, 1904, p. 164 f.).

What are the facts? In the first Epistle of his which has come down to us, which is also the first extant New Testament writing—1 Thessalonians—written from Corinth about A.D. 51, St. Paul simply asserts the fact of the Resurrection without defining its nature. He recalls how the Thessalonians "turned unto God from idols, to serve a living and true God, and to wait for his Son from heaven, whom he raised from the dead, even Jesus" (i. 9 f.); "if we believe that Jesus died and rose again, even so," etc. (iv. 14). The fact is referred to incidentally as if it were a matter unquestioned in the Church. This is St. Paul's general attitude in his Epistles, and it is an attitude even more significant as an attestation of the Resurrection than any more direct evidence.

But St. Paul's conception of the nature of the fact is plainly indicated by the more explicit reference in 1 Cor. xv., written about the year A.D. 55 (see Sanday, in *Encycl. Biblica*, i. 904), *i.e.*, about twenty-five years after the Resurrection. Here St. Paul reminds the Corinthians of the fundamental facts of his preaching and of their faith—"the gospel which I preached unto you . . . by which also ye are saved" (ver. 1 f.). In this earliest extant narrative of the facts, which is therefore the primary document in regard to the Resurrection, St. Paul's words are: "For I delivered unto you first of all (ἐν πρώτοις, "first and foremost" [Moffatt]) that which also I received, how that Christ died for our sins according to the scriptures; and that he was buried; and that he hath been raised on the third day according to the scriptures; and that he appeared to Cephas," etc. (ver. 3 ff.). In this outline statement of the substance of his preaching in Corinth the following points of importance are to be noted:

(1) St. Paul explicitly refers to a rising "on the third day," which was distinct from and preparatory to the appearances. This event on the third day, as concrete an event as the death of Jesus, is set over against the burial, and is presented as the reversal of it, thus making clear what is meant by the fact. If St. Paul meant simply a spiritual resurrection, a manifestation of the spirit of Jesus from heaven, he need have said no more than that Jesus died and on the third day appeared to the disciples. The clause "and that he was buried" not merely emphasizes the full reality of His death, but points to the grave as the state from which the Resur-

rection took place. "Why mention His *burial* unless it
was His bodily resurrection he [Paul] had in view?"
(Dods, in *Supernatural Christianity*, p. 103). Who
ever heard of a spirit being buried? Even Schmiedel
somewhat inconsistently admits this: "That Jesus was
buried and that 'he has been raised' (1 Cor. xv. 4)
cannot be affirmed by any one who has not the reanimation of the body in mind" (*Encycl. Biblica*, iv. 4059). So
in the other two passages in St. Paul's writings where
reference is made to the burial of our Lord (Rom. vi. 4 ;
Col. ii. 12). In both, the Resurrection is presented as
relative to the burial and as the reversal of it, showing
that even if St. Paul does not explicitly mention the
empty grave it was the bodily resurrection he had in
view. This is borne out by the whole line of the
Apostle's argument in 1 Cor. xv. St. Paul is replying
to those in Corinth who denied, not the continued
spiritual existence of the Christian after death, but the
possibility of his bodily resurrection, on the ground that
they could not conceive how the body could rise; and
he does so by setting the resurrection of Christian
believers, the quickening of their mortal bodies
(ver. 42 ff.), in closest and organic connexion with the
resurrection of Christ as "the firstfruits of them that
are asleep" (ver. 20). Here, obviously, only a reference
to the bodily resurrection of our Lord would have been
relevant. This is the conception of the Resurrection
which permeates his Epistles (*e.g.*, Rom. vi. 4 ff., viii. 11 ;
2 Cor. v. 1–5 ; Phil. iii. 21), and it is reflected in the
speeches of St. Paul reported in the Acts (xiii. 29 f.,
xvii. 31, xxvi. 23). Such a conception of the Resurrec-

tion, indeed, was required by the whole context of Pauline thought on the matter. For St. Paul, as for the entire Jewish Christian community, sin and physical death stood in organic connexion with each other. Hence Christ's triumph over sin involved for him His final and complete victory over the death not only of the soul but of the body as well.

(2) The significance of the term used in reference to the resurrection of Christ has to be noted as setting forth St. Paul's conception of the nature of the event. He does not say simply, " He rose on the third day," but, " He hath been raised (ἐγήγερται) on the third day." The use of the perfect tense signifies that the event was of such a character as had an abiding effect on the condition of the Lord. His resurrection was not like other raisings from the dead recorded in the Scriptures, where the raising meant simply restoration to the old life and the old conditions, with the prospect of meeting death again in the future. Christ rose, St. Paul says, and remains in the risen state; He has triumphed over death: " Christ being raised from the dead dieth no more; death no more hath dominion over him " (Rom. vi. 9). As risen He belongs to a new and higher mode of being. St. Paul's conception of the nature of Christ's risen body is more fully elucidated by his teaching as regards the " spiritual " body (see below, Chap. VI.).

(3) This gospel which he had preached in Corinth, including as one of its great affirmations the fact that Christ was raised on the third day, was not, he says, peculiar or original to him. He had but " delivered "

(παρέδωκα, "passed on" [Moffatt]) what he had himself
"received" (παρέλαβον)—received not by direct revelation
from Christ, but through tradition from those who
were in Christ before him (see Lake, *The Historical
Evidence for the Resurrection of Jesus Christ*, p. 38 ff.).
The channel through which he received the tradition he
does not here indicate.   In the Epistle to the Galatians,
however, an Epistle accepted with practical unanimity
by New Testament scholars though it is difficult to date
it definitely, he tells us that three years after his
conversion he went up to Jerusalem expressly "to visit
Cephas" (i. 18, ἱστορῆσαι Κηφᾶν), that he stayed there
for a fortnight, and that he saw St. James also.   The
term ἱστορῆσαι "implies a careful and searching inquiry
on his [Paul's] part" (A. Edersheim, *Life and Times of
Jesus the Messiah*[4], London, 1887, ii. 625 ; cf. Knowling,
Testimony of St. Paul to Christ, p. 222, and A. Sabatier,
The Apostle Paul, Eng. tr., London, 1891, p. 81).
That his knowledge of the details of the common
Christian tradition may be traced to this visit and
prolonged interview with two of the primary witnesses
of the Resurrection is, therefore, altogether probable.
As Schmiedel acknowledges, "during his fifteen days'
visit to Peter and James (Gal. i. 18 f.), he had the
best opportunity to perfect his knowledge on the
subject in the most authentic manner" (*ut sup.* iv.
4057).

Through this visit, therefore, if not indeed already
at his conversion, he came into possession of the
facts which he had handed on to the Corinthians as
the common Christian tradition.   Some hold (*e.g.,*

W. Bousset, *Kyrios Christos*, Göttingen, 1913, p. 92 ff.) that the tradition which St. Paul here repeats, though indirectly derived from the older apostles, was mediated for him by the Hellenistic Christianity of Damascus and Antioch, and suffered modification accordingly. But St. Paul distinctly asserts (ver. 11) that the substance of his preaching in Corinth was identical with that of the other apostles. This is a fact of the first importance. St. Paul's conversion took place not long after the death of Christ. Lightfoot dated it six or seven years after the Crucifixion, but the trend of more recent criticism is to place it much earlier, within a year or two of this event. Harnack places it in the year following the Death, as do also McGiffert and Moffatt, though Ramsay makes it three or four and Weizsäcker five years after (see art. " Chronology of the New Testament " in Hastings' *Dict. of Bible,* i. 424). St. Paul's visit to Jerusalem, therefore, and his interview with St. Peter and St. James fall possibly within five years, but certainly well within ten years, of the Resurrection. We have, accordingly, in documents which all reasonable critics admit, the clearest evidence as to what the fundamental facts of Christianity were, as taught in the primitive community, within the first decade of the event, by those who were primary witnesses of the Resurrection. These were, that " Christ died for our sins, according to the scriptures," that " he was buried," that " on the third day he was raised from the dead according to the scriptures," and that " he appeared " to His disciples. If St. Paul's testimony, therefore, proves anything, it proves that the earliest apostolic witness included not only the fact of

appearances of the Risen Christ, but the empty grave
and the Resurrection on the third day.

(4) One other point in St. Paul's summary statement
is to be noted. The atoning death of Christ ("for our
sins") and His resurrection on the third day are represented as being "according to the scriptures" (κατὰ τὰς
γραφάς, ver. 3 f.). St. Paul's belief in the Resurrection
on the third day has been represented as a deduction or
inference from Old Testament prophetic Scripture, based
"on theological rather than historical grounds" (Lake,
Resurrection of Jesus Christ, p. 264), or as due to a
"Messianic dogmatic," a pre-Christian sketch of the Christ-
portrait derived from widespread non-Jewish myths(chiefly
Babylonian in origin) and embodied in Jewish writings
(see, *e.g.*, T. K. Cheyne, *Bible Problems*, London, 1904,
p. 113). In answer to this it is sufficient here to note
that St. Paul claims to stand in this matter precisely on
the same ground as the earlier apostles. The gospel he
had preached to the Corinthians in its two great affirmations—the atoning significance of the Death and the
reality of the Resurrection on the third day—was not,
he claims, original to him; he had but "handed on" the
tradition which he had himself "received." The attempt
to explain the primitive apostolic belief in the Resurrection on the third day as an inference from Scripture will
be considered later (below, p. 57 ff.).

(b) *The Appearings of the Risen Christ*

St. Paul's witness to the Resurrection includes, however, not only the empty grave on the third day but the

fact of subsequent appearings[1] of the Risen Lord. In his outline statement in 1 Cor. xv. the following list of Appearings is given: "He appeared to Cephas; then to the twelve; after that he appeared to over five hundred brethren at once, the majority of whom survive to this day though some have died; after that he appeared to James, then to all the apostles, and last of all he appeared to me also—this so-called 'abortion' of an apostle" (vers. 5–8). In this statement several things have to be observed.

(1) The purpose for which St. Paul adduced this list has to be noted, for the consideration of this at once removes certain objections which have been urged against it. There were some members of the Corinthian Church (τινές, ver. 12) who denied the fact of the resurrection of the dead—not the resurrection of Jesus in particular, but the resurrection of the dead generally. They said, "There is no such thing as a resurrection of dead persons" (ἀνάστασις νεκρῶν οὐκ ἔστιν, ver. 12; cf. ver. 29, "dead men are not raised at all" [ὅλως]), asserting a universal negative. Who these τινές were St. Paul does not say, but we know that in his missionary labours among the Greeks the subject of teaching which proved the chief stumbling-block was the resurrection of the dead. In Athens, e.g., we are told that, when he began to speak of the resurrection of dead men (ἀνάστασιν νεκρῶν), they derided the very idea, and their manifest

---

[1] We prefer in general to speak of the "appearings" rather than of the "appearances" of Jesus after the Resurrection, the latter term suggesting phenomena of a ghostly or apparitional character, which, as we shall see, is not the New Testament representation.

impatience and ridicule forced him to terminate his speech abruptly (Acts xvii. 32; cf. xxvi. 8). These τινές in Corinth shared the prejudice of Greek culture against the idea of a bodily resurrection. They denied the possibility of the fact. They repeated the dogma "Dead men do not rise" as the last word of philosophy, much as in modern times the similar dogma "Miracles do not happen" has been repeated as the last word of science.

To deny the resurrection of the dead, however, is by implication to deny Christ's resurrection, and to do this is to contravene the Gospel witness, and, further, as St. Paul shows by the *reductio ad absurdum* argument, to render the whole saving worth of the gospel ineffective (vers. 14–18), and to show that they believed the gospel heedlessly or at haphazard (εἰκῇ, ver. 2) without seriously realizing the facts involved. So, before advancing to the doctrinal discussion which was the real purpose of his argument in this great chapter, St. Paul felt called to rehearse the historical evidence for Christ's bodily resurrection which he had "received," and which he had already "delivered" to them by word of mouth when he was among them. In this rehearsal he recalled not only the Burial and the fact of the Resurrection on the third day, but a summary of the chief appearings of the Lord after His resurrection. Whether St. Paul is here giving his own summarized statement of the principal witnesses to the Resurrection or, as some maintain, a stereotyped or formulated summary list which he had himself received and had handed on to the Corinthians ("a selection made for purposes of preaching" [Sanday, Hastings' *Dict. of Bible*, ii. 640ᵃ]) does not affect the argument. In either case the list given is a summary statement of evidence already received.

The remembrance of this supplies a complete answer to the objections drawn from St. Paul's omitting to refer to certain Appearings recorded in the Gospels. Weizsäcker, *e.g.*, argues from St. Paul's silence as to the Appearing to the women at the grave, recorded in the Gospels, and from his placing the Appearing to St. Peter first in his list of Christophanies, to his ignorance of the fact. "The only possible explanation is that the Apostle was ignorant of its existence" (*Apost. Age²*, i. 5). And from this he proceeds to draw the inference that, since "Paul's knowledge of these things must have come from the heads of the primitive Church, therefore it is the primitive Church itself that was ignorant of any such tradition," which is, therefore, a "later product" (p. 6). Such is the conclusion to which Weizsäcker comes on the supposition on which he proceeds that St. Paul is here relating the Appearings "in order to prove the fact" of the Resurrection, "proof which he undertakes so earnestly and carries out with such precision" (p. 5). To like effect Schmiedel: "By his careful enumeration with 'then . . . next . . . next . . . then . . . lastly' (εἶτα . . . ἔπειτα . . . ἔπειτα . . . εἶτα . . . ἔσχατον, xv. 5–8) he guarantees not only chronological order but also completeness" (*Encycl. Bibl.* iv. 4058). On this ground he argues, like Weizsäcker, from St. Paul's omission of reference to the Appearing to the women to his ignorance of the fact, and hence to the supposition that the Jerusalem Church, from which St. Paul derived his facts, included in its testimony to the Resurrection no such stories of the appearing of Jesus to the women as are now found in the Gospels.

Now it is doubtless a fair inference from St. Paul's form of statement that he gives the Appearings which he mentions in what he considers their chronological order. So much "then . . . after that . . .," etc., denotes or implies. But there is nothing to show that he considers his enumeration exhaustive. Indeed, there is everything against it. St. Paul, it has to be remembered, is not here attempting to prove the resurrection of Christ. That was not in doubt. He starts from that as a fact accepted by his correspondents in Corinth —part of the Gospel which they had "received" (ver. 1) —and arguing from that he seeks to convince those among them who doubted of their own resurrection. It is not in St. Paul's mind, therefore, to give an exhaustive list of the appearings of Christ after His resurrection, much less as Schmiedel represents, to present "every possible argument" for the fact (*ut sup.* iv. 4057). He is content to recall briefly the main facts which he had already "delivered" to them, and which were part of the Christian tradition which he himself had "received" after his conversion. The statement here given is almost as condensed as it could possibly be, and it is difficult to see how it could ever be mistaken for an exhaustive evidential account of the proofs of Christ's resurrection. In this list nothing more than the names or numbers of the witnesses are given. No mention is made of locality or other detail of the Appearings, not from lack of knowledge but because the Corinthians themselves would be able to fill in the details from memory. The passage is but a recapitulation of oral teaching, giving in a summary fashion what he had enlarged upon in all its circumstances and significance when he was among them. For this summary purpose St. Paul selects the Appearings to the leaders of the Church whose names were well known to the Corinthians and would carry weight with them, and who were, like himself, specially chosen and commissioned to be witnesses of the Resurrection (1 Cor. xv. 15; cf. Acts i. 22, iv. 33)—Cephas, the Twelve, St. James, all the apostles—mentioning, besides these, only the great crowning manifestation of the Risen Lord to "more than five hundred brethren at once." This in itself would explain the omission of the Appearing to the women which had a more private significance and would not be of special interest to the Corinthians. It may have been on this ground too, as Sanday suggests (Hastings' *Dict. of Bible*, ii. 639ᵇ)—"because the two disciples involved were not otherwise conspicuous as active preachers or prominent leaders"—that the Appearing on the way to Emmaus is not mentioned. In any case, the mere omission to mention this Appearing or that to the women cannot by itself be held to argue St. Paul's ignorance of the fact (though this was possible), much less warrant the conclusion that the manifestation of Jesus to the women had no place in the primitive Church tradition.

(2) Whether St. Paul means that the entire list of Appearings here given (with the exception, of course, of that to himself) formed part of the original tradition which he had received has been disputed. The grammatical construction continues unbroken to the end of

ver. 5 ("that he hath been raised on the third day . . . and that he appeared to Cephas, then to the twelve") and then changes ("then he appeared," etc.): and some hold that these later Appearings were added to the list by St. Paul himself.   But it is precarious to make the mere grammatical structure of the sentence the basis of reasoning.   Such a break is not unusual with St. Paul. Certainly the implied idea would seem to be that St. Paul is here summarizing the common tradition which he had received, and it is natural to suppose that the recapitulation extends to the end of the series.   Chase interprets the break in construction, if intentional, as denoting that "the Apostle regards the appearances which he mentions as falling into two groups," and infers that "he places the appearance to Cephas and that to the Twelve among the events 'of the third day'" (*Gospels in the Light of Hist. Criticism*, p. 41).

A detailed examination of St. Paul's summary list will show how far it is in line with the Gospel accounts and confirms the narratives there given.

(i.) "He appeared to Cephas." The source of St. Paul's knowledge of this Appearing is scarcely open to dispute.   When he went up to Jerusalem to "visit Cephas," who can doubt that while St. Paul had much to say of his experiences on the Damascus road St. Peter told how the Master had appeared to himself on the very day of the Resurrection.   Of the Evangelists, Luke alone mentions this Appearing and assigns to Peter the privilege of being the first apostle to whom the Risen Lord appeared (xxiv. 34).   The source of Luke's knowledge is not difficult to trace.

(ii.) "Then to the twelve." "The twelve" is here used as the official title of the apostolic body—a technical phrase (cf. Godet, *in loc.*; Lake, *Resurrection of Jesus Christ*, p. 37)—without exact regard to number.   It is probable that the incident to which St. Paul here refers was the Appearing to the Ten in the Upper Chamber on the evening of the Resurrection (Luke xxiv. 36; John xx. 19), or the

Appearing to the Eleven (Thomas being present) a week later (John xx. 26) ; or it may be that St. Paul's reference would cover both these incidents. It is the fact of the manifestation of the Lord to the assembled company of His selected companions that is referred to, and the absence of Thomas on the day of the Resurrection is an accident. Accordingly, even if others were present on the first of these occasions, as Luke's language seems to imply ("the eleven and those that were with them," ver. 33), the significance of the Appearing would rest in the recognition of the Lord by His chosen friends.

(iii.) "Then he appeared to above five hundred brethren once for all" (ἐφάπαξ)—rather than "at once" or "simultaneously" (cf. Rom. vi. 10 ; Acts vii. 27, ix. 12, x. 10)—the implication of ἐφάπαξ being that not only did they see the Lord together but "the occasion in question was the only one on which this large company of disciples had so wonderful an experience" (*Church Quarterly Review*, lxi. [1906] 328). The identity of this Appearing with that on a mountain in Galilee recorded in Matt. xxviii. 16 f.—the Appearing foretold in the promise of vers. 7, 10 and anticipated in Mark xvi. 7—has been maintained by many. And certainly this Appearing would seem to require location in Galilee, not in Jerusalem. "An appearance to so large a body of disciples at one time could only have taken place on the Galilean hills" (Swete, *Appearances of our Lord after the Passion*, p. 82). Matthew, indeed, speaks only of "the eleven disciples" in connexion with this meeting in Galilee, but in the expression "some doubted" (οἱ δὲ ἐδίστασαν, Matt. xxviii. 17) there has been found an indirect indication of the presence of a larger body. "In the small body of the eleven there is hardly room for a 'some'" (Orr, *Resurrection of Jesus*, p. 190). Further, as H. Latham (*Risen Master*, Cambridge, 1901, p. 290) urges, a meeting with the Eleven only would not have necessitated an appointment in the hill country. It could have been held with perfect safety in a room at Capernaum. Matthew's speaking only of "the eleven disciples" in connexion with the meeting may be explained by the fact that his interest lay wholly in the commission of the Risen Lord to the apostles which was given at this meeting (cf. Chase, *Gospels in the Light of Hist. Criticism*, p. 42). The identification can never indeed be more than a probability. Weiss (*in loc.*) rejects it, and E. von Dobschütz (*Ostern und Pfingsten*, Leipzig, 1903, p. 34), followed by Harnack and Lake, attempts to identify the Appearing with the coming down of the Holy Spirit upon the assembled company on the Day of Pentecost. But in any case it is to be noted that St. Paul, writing twenty-five years after the Resurrection, says that the majority of those "more than five hundred" were still living and could be interrogated by his readers for themselves as he had doubtless interrogated them. Of this Appearing the Apostle makes much, including it even in a summary list; as well indeed he might, for, even if the Eleven could be deceived or deceivers, was it credible that their error or their fraud would be shared by so large a company? "Some there must have been among them who, as the days went on, would have exposed the imposture or betrayed their doubts. But if any doubts of this kind had arisen, it would have been dangerous for the Apostle to appeal to the survivors of the five hundred in a letter written to Corinth, where he had enemies who were in frequent communication with Jerusalem" (Swete, *Appearances*, p. 83 f.).

(iv.) "Then he appeared to James." Of this Appearing we have no notice in the Gospels. An extra-canonical account of it is found in the fragment of the *Gospel according to the Hebrews* preserved by Jerome (*de Vir. Ill.* 2), a Palestinian work of the end of the first or beginning of the second century. "The Lord . . . went to James and appeared to him; for James had sworn that he would not eat bread from the hour in which he had drunk the cup of the Lord until he saw Him raised from the dead. . . . Bring, the Lord said, a table and bread. . . . He brought bread, and (Jesus) blessed and brake it and gave it to James the Just and said to him, My brother, eat thy bread, for the Son of Man has risen from the dead." This cannot, however, "with any confidence be connected with the appearance to James the Lord's brother of which S. Paul speaks" (Swete, p. 89 f.; cf. J. B. Mayor, *Epistle of St. James*[3], London, 1910, p. xxvii). Though not thus referred to elsewhere in the New Testament, corroboration of the fact may be derived from the light thrown by it on what we are told of the Lord's brothers after the Resurrection. That they did not believe in Him during the days of His public ministry is recorded in the Fourth Gospel (John vii. 5; cf. Mark iii. 21). After the Ascension, however, we find them included among the little company of believers (Acts i. 14); and within a short time we find St. James in particular president of the Jerusalem Church (Acts xv. 13). The natural explanation of the change is contained in St. Paul's assertion "He appeared to James." It seems impossible to doubt that St. Paul derived his information direct from St. James himself during his fortnight's visit to Jerusalem (Gal. i. 18); and this Appearing is included in the summary because of the special value attached to the testimony of St. James from the fact that he was the eldest brother of the Lord and head of the Jerusalem Mother Church, as well as from the fact of his previous unbelief.

(v.) "Then to all the apostles." The Appearings in this list being set down, as seems likely, in chronological order, the incident to which St. Paul here refers may with a reasonable degree of probability be identified with the appearing of Christ to the Eleven before the Ascension, more circumstantially narrated by Luke (xxiv. 50 f.; Acts i. 6 f.; cf. Mark xvi. 14 f.). Acts i. 22, which speaks of those who had companied with the Eleven from the beginning until "the day that he was received up," would support the contention of those who hold that on the occasion of this Appearing others were present besides the Eleven, and that St. Paul means to convey this by distinguishing an Appearing to "all the apostles" from an Appearing to "the twelve." St. Paul's wider usage of the term ἀπόστολος makes such an interpretation possible.

The Appearings recorded by St. Paul may thus be held to correspond to Appearings recorded in the Gospels, with the one exception of that to St. James, which we have seen reason to assume he obtained at first hand during his visit to Jerusalem. The further Appearings of the Risen Christ recorded in the Gospels of which there is no mention in St. Paul's summary—the Appearing to the women, to Mary Magdalene, to the travellers to Emmaus, to the seven at the Sea of Tiberias—may have been omitted for the reason already indicated, viz. that they were of less interest for the purpose in view, having little more than a private significance. St. Paul's list, therefore, helps us to verify, and at one or two points to supplement, the narrative of the Gospels. The significance of this has to be noted. It has often been asserted that the Gospel story of the Resurrection was not committed to writing till thirty or forty years after

the events recorded, and that this period allows time
for the incorporation of details which may be nothing
more than tradition.   But here we have written down
within twenty-two or twenty-three years of the event
(taking the date of 1 Cor. as A.D. 55) a list of witnesses
expressly affirmed to be part of the tradition which St.
Paul had received either at his conversion (A.D. 31 or 33)
or, at latest, during his visit to Jerusalem three years
later, from first-hand sources, thus taking us back to
within a few years of the event.   And how remarkable
a list it is—" Cephas," " James," " the twelve," " more
than five hundred brethren," and " all the apostles."
To realize the weight of this testimony it must be taken
as a whole and not in its isolated parts.   The number
and variety of the persons to whom the manifestations
were made, as well as the character and status of the
witnesses and the simultaneous perception by many,
make this a statement of evidence for the Resurrection
which cannot be made light of by the impartial historian.

(3) The most important Appearing of all, as giving
St. Paul's direct evidence to the Resurrection—an
addition to the traditional list " received "—has yet
to be considered.   Behind St. Paul's preaching of the
Resurrection there stood not only the testimony of others,
but the great historical fact of the Risen Lord's appearing
to himself on the way to Damascus.   " Last of all
(ἔσχατον πάντων) he appeared also to me—to this
so-called ' abortion ' of an apostle " (ὡσπερεὶ τῷ
ἐκτρώματι, ver. 8).

The Authorized Version translation "as to one born out of due
time" finds the suggestion in ὡσπερεὶ τῷ ἐκτρώματι to be that he

was born too late to witness one of the normal appearings of Christ after the Resurrection and before the Ascension. But J. Weiss points out (H. A. W. Meyer, *Kommentar über das Neue Testament*, "Der erste Korintherbrief," Göttingen, 1910, *in loc.*) that ἔκτρωμα means born not too late but too early, too quickly, the suggestion being that of the suddenness and violence of St. Paul's birth into Christ. His was an unripe and violent birth (cf. G. G. Findlay, *Expos. Gk. Test.*, "1 Cor.," London, 1900, *in loc.*, "the unripe birth of one who was changed at a stroke from the persecutor into the Apostle, instead of maturing normally for his work"). In either case the point is the abnormality of St. Paul's birth into faith and apostleship, and probably the significance of the article is, as Weiss points out, that τὸ ἔκτρωμα was an insulting epithet flung at St. Paul by those who belittled his apostleship. In their eyes he was a real *Missgeburt*. St. Paul adopts the title and gives it a deeper meaning, arguing that, notwithstanding his abnormality and unworthiness, his apostleship was as valid as that of the older apostles.

A considerable body of negative criticism has maintained that the Appearing to St. Paul was of an inward visionary character, and that, since he includes it in his list with the others without any discrimination between them except as regards time, using the same word (ὤφθη) to describe all the Appearings, he must have regarded these as like his own, visionary. Weizsäcker, *e.g.*, says: "There is absolutely no proof that Paul presupposed a physical Christophany in the case of the older Apostles. Had he done so he could not have put his own experience on a level with theirs. But since he does this, we must conclude that he looked upon the visions of his predecessors in the same light as his own" (*Apost. Age*[2], i. 9 ; cf. O. Pfleiderer, *Christian Origins*, Eng. tr., London, 1906, pp. 136 f., 160 f.). The "more materialistic" accounts of the Appearings given in the Gospels are the outcome of later "un-

historical embellishments." The truth, however, is, as
Westcott points out (*Gospel of the Resurrection*, p. 111),
that the exact converse is the proper line of argument.
St. Paul, we have seen, conceived of the Resurrection as
a bodily Resurrection, in this believing himself to be at
one with the older apostles, and his use of the same
term to describe all the Appearings shows that he
regarded the Appearing of the Risen Lord to himself
on the road to Damascus as of the same kind as those
granted to the others—less tangible it may be, but not
less objective. He believed, and always acted on the
belief, that he had seen the Risen Lord in the same
sense as did those who saw Him during the forty days,
that he was a witness of Christ's resurrection in the
same sense as the others were, and the last of such
witnesses; and this " seeing " he regarded as containing
the basis and justification of his apostolic mission. He
claimed to be as directly commissioned by our Lord in
person as any other of the apostles (Gal. i. 11–17).
" Am I not an apostle, have I not seen Jesus our Lord ? "
(οὐχὶ Ἰησοῦν τὸν Κύριον ἡμῶν ἑώρακα, 1 Cor. ix. 1)
(cf. John xx. 18, ἑώρακε τὸν Κύριον; ver. 25, ἑωράκαμεν
τὸν Κύριον; ver. 29, ἑωράκάς με). " The phrase seems
to have been current in the Apostolic Church in speaking of a personal experience of the appearances of the
risen Christ " (Swete, *Appearances*, p. 41 n.). That the
reference here is to a risen Appearing and not to a
seeing of Jesus during His earthly life is obvious. For
even if, as some maintain, St. Paul had so seen the Lord,
what he is concerned with in this passage is his claim to
be an apostle and a witness equally with the Twelve of

the Lord's resurrection; and to justify this claim a "seeing" of the Risen Lord was necessary.

The visionary character of this experience has sometimes been argued from the mere use of the term ὤφθη, but this is illegitimate. The term is, indeed, sometimes used of "visionary" (e.g. Acts xvi. 9); but it is used equally of seeing which is not visionary (e.g. Acts vii. 26). "What it suggests in almost every case is the idea of something sudden or unexpected; that which is seen is conceived to be so, not because one is looking at it or for it, but because it has unexpectedly thrust itself upon the sight" (Denney, *Jesus and the Gospel*, p. 116). Support for the visionary interpretation of the Appearing has, however, been sought by reference to St. Paul's words elsewhere.

Two passages in particular have been adduced: 2 Cor. xii. 1–9; Gal. i. 15 f. To take the latter first: "When it was the good pleasure of God, who separated me even from my mother's womb, and called me through his grace, to reveal his Son in me (ἐν ἐμοί), that I might preach him among the Gentiles." That this revelation refers to his experience near Damascus is indicated in ver. 17; and it is urged that in these words St. Paul unequivocally asserts the inward character of the revelation granted to him, and that this meaning must in consequence be applied to all other passages in his writings where the point is spoken of. But St. Paul's assertion here of the inward character of the revelation does not require us to resolve the whole manifestation into an inward experience and exclude an accompanying or preceding appearance vouchsafed to the senses.

Lightfoot (*in loc.*) maintains that the words, "when it pleased God to reveal his Son in me," should be taken in close connexion with the words immediately following, "that I might preach him among the Gentiles" (this giving the content of the inner and spiritual revelation); while the words, "called me by his grace," should be understood as a reference to the actual event on the Damascus road on which the inner revelation supervened. However this may be, the admission of an inner revelation does not exclude an external manifestation as well. Even such a negative critic as Meyer admits this: "It is not therefore (because of the inward revelation) to be denied that Paul conceived the appearance of Christ to him to be objective and external" (*Die Auferstehung Christi*, p. 186). The revelation of God to him was two-fold, the inward supplementing the outward. Such an inward revelation indeed, as Knowling points out, was necessary to complete and interpret the outward. Without this "the outward appearance could never have been recognised for what it was in its full meaning, nor could the Apostle have been assured against all suspicion of an illusion of the senses" (*Testimony of St. Paul*, p. 184). The outer revelation separated from the inner would have been valueless, and would have left St. Paul in the same bewildered state as the companions of his journey. But the outward revelation, though valueless without the inward, was a necessary condition and presupposition of it (cf. Lietzmann, *Handbuch zum N.T.*, Tübingen, 1900, *in loc.*).

In the other passage referred to, 2 Cor. xii. 1 ff., St. Paul writes, "I must needs glory, though it is not expedient; but I will come to visions and revelations of the Lord," etc. May not the Apostle, it is urged, have "seen" the Lord in one of these ecstatic visions, visions with regard to which he could not even affirm whether he was in the body or out of it? But this very passage, as Sabatier truly observes, "shows that Paul, so far from comparing the manifestation of Christ to him at his conversion with the visions he afterwards enjoyed, laid down an essential difference between them" (*The Apostle Paul*, p. 65). Of the latter he speaks with the utmost reserve and reticence—"of which it is not expedient that he should glory." But the former he places in the forefront of his preaching, as containing not only the grounds of his conversion, but, as we have seen, the basis of his claim to apostleship. Moreover, St. Paul describes the appearing of Christ here referred to as the last of a series—"last of all" (ἔσχατον πάντων). The force of the words is often overlooked. They do not mean merely that St. Paul was the last of the particular series of persons named in the previous verses; "he does not say . . . that Christ appeared to him the last; but that He appeared to him for the last time, *i.e.* as in a series which was now closed" (Knowling, p. 182). St. Paul, we know, had many visions and revelations of the Lord after this, and he could not therefore tell us more definitely than he does by this expression "last of all" how fully and clearly he distinguished between the Damascus vision and every other vision of the Risen Saviour (cf. Weiss, on 1 Cor. xv. 8 : " All later visions of Christ belong for Paul to a different category, they cannot be viewed in the same way as proofs of the Resurrection ").

This external objective character of the appearing
of the Risen Christ to St. Paul is corroborated by an
examination of the three accounts of it given in Acts
(ix. 1–22, xxii. 1–16, xxvi. 1–18). The first occurs in
the course of Luke's own narrative of the circumstances
of St. Paul's conversion. The second occurs in the
report of St. Paul's defence before Lysias, when Luke
was probably present (a " we " section). The third is in
the report of St. Paul's defence before Agrippa, when
Luke again was probably present. Of these different
accounts Schmiedel says that " they contradict one
another so violently . . . that it is difficult to imagine
how it could ever have been possible for an author to
take them up into his book in their present forms "
(*Encycl. Bibl.* iv. 4063). The divergences, however,
relate to details, not to the essential facts. " In the
essential point there is the same impression throughout "
(H. Weinel, *St. Paul*, Eng. tr., London, 1906, p. 77).

The chief variations concern (i.) the effect of the Appearing
upon St. Paul's companions : in the first account they are described
as "hearing the voice but beholding no man " (ix. 7, ἀκούοντες μὲν τῆς
φωνῆς, μηδένα δὲ θεωροῦντες) ; in the second it is said, " They beheld
indeed the light, but heard not the voice of him that spake to me "
(xxii. 9, τὴν δὲ φωνὴν οὐκ ἤκουσαν τοῦ λαλοῦντός μοι) ; (ii.) the place
of Ananias : in the first account Saul is bidden to arise and go into
the city, where it shall be told him what he must do. So also in
the second account. The instruction is then left to be given by
Ananias. But in the third account the instruction is given by the
Lord Himself and no mention is made of Ananias. These variations,
however, are relatively unimportant. As regards (i.), in the very
variation a significance has been discerned. " They may have
heard a vague sound (φωνῆς, genitive), and yet not the articulate,
intelligible voice (φωνήν, accusative), which fell upon St. Paul's
ear with a definite meaning " (H. A. A. Kennedy, *St. Paul's Conceptions of the Last Things*, London, 1904, p. 86 ; cf. Grimm-Thayer,

s.v.). As regards (ii.), St. Paul's omission in Acts xxvi. of the part of Ananias may be sufficiently explained by the difference of circumstances. He naturally dwelt on it in his defence before a Jewish mob (Acts xxii.), because the mention of Ananias and his part would be reassuring to his hearers, while in speaking before Festus and Agrippa at Cæsarea such a reference would be uncalled for. In Acts ix. we have the historian's own circumstantial narrative of the course of events where we would expect Ananias to be mentioned.

In regard to St. Paul's own experience of the Appearing the different accounts agree in the following details. (i.) A light from heaven suddenly shone round about him as he journeyed to Damascus (ix. 3, περιήστραψεν φῶς; xxii. 6, περιαστράψαι φῶς; xxvi. 13, περιλάμψαν . . . φῶς). Of this light Saul's fellow-travellers also were cognizant. (ii.) From the shock of this dazzling light Saul falls prostrate on the ground. (iii.) He hears a voice (the others heard only a sound), which he discovers to be that of the Glorified Jesus speaking to him in words which he can understand. Whether, besides seeing a splendour of light and hearing a voice, St. Paul saw also the Risen Lord in bodily form the accounts in Acts do not explicitly assert—though this seems implied in what is said by contrast of the experience of his companions, who are described as hearing the voice but "beholding no man" (μηδένα θεωροῦντες, Acts ix. 7), and in Barnabas' subsequent announcement to the Church at Jerusalem that "Saul had seen the Lord in the way" (Acts ix. 27; cf. his announcement to St. Paul himself, "the Lord, even Jesus, who appeared unto thee," ver. 17; cf. xxii. 14).

That St. Paul believed he had seen the Lord in His risen body is involved in the references to the event in his letter to Corinth which we have already considered (1 Cor. ix. 1, xv. 8). In the former passage, in defending his apostleship he claims to have "seen Jesus Christ our Lord." The primary apostolic function was to witness to the resurrection of Christ, and in order to discharge this function it was requisite that the Apostle should with his own eyes have seen the Risen Lord. In the latter passage, in which he classes his own experience with the earlier appearings of the Risen Christ, his purpose is to prove not the continued spiritual existence of the Christian, but his bodily resurrection; and only a reference to the bodily resurrection of our Lord and a bodily appearing would have been relevant. But according to the account in Acts the aspect of the appearance which chiefly impressed him was the Divine glory of it, "the glory of that light" (Acts xxii. 11). And this is reflected in many passages in his letters— e.g. 2 Thess. i. 9–11, ii. 8; 1 Cor. xv. 44–49; Rom. viii. 18, 29; 1 Tim. vi. 15 f.; 2 Tim. i. 10 f., and especially Phil. iii. 20 f. ("the body of his glory"). The vision he saw was of Christ glorified; but this Glorified Christ was identical with the Crucified Jesus of Nazareth (Acts xxii. 8, "I am Jesus of Nazareth, whom thou persecutest"; xxvi. 15, "I am Jesus whom thou persecutest"). And, however the phenomena perceived by his senses were to be described, what is important to note is the immediate effect that the Appearing had upon him, for St. Paul himself in his accounts of it is concerned with the significance of the fact rather than with any precise descriptive details. He became, through it, absolutely convinced that the Jesus who was crucified and whose followers he was persecuting was indeed the Risen and Exalted Lord (Κύριος); and this conviction revolutionized his whole thought and life, energizing in him unto a new life of absolute devotion and surrender whereby he became henceforth the property (δοῦλος) of a crucified but living and glorified Christ (Rom. i. 1 ; Gal. i. 10 ; Phil. i. 1). His own explanation of the transformation is contained in these words, "He appeared to me also"—words in which he claimed for himself the same kind of revelation as that made to Peter, James, and the other apostles after the Resurrection.

Various attempts have been made to explain the Appearing on purely natural grounds. Any explanation, to be satisfactory, must be able to give a sufficient reason for the greatness of the revolutionary change referred to in the persecutor's experience, with its lasting moral and spiritual effects.

(i.) Taken to this test, the attempt to account for the experience as a species of epileptic seizure in scorching heat, the product of excitable nerves and atmospheric effects—a view identified with the name of Renan (cf., more recently, Weinel, *St. Paul*, p. 82 f.)—is at once condemned as inadequate.

(ii.) W. James speaks of a form of "sensory automatism" which he calls a "photism," a "hallucinatory or pseudo-hallucinatory" phenomenon, and represents St. Paul's "blinding heavenly vision" as a phenomenon of this sort (*Varieties of Religious Experience*, London, 1902, p. 251 f.). The parallelism between St. Paul's experience and the modern instances quoted is hard to find, but inasmuch as James himself claims that his hypothesis does not necessarily involve a denial of the heavenly or Divine origin of the appearance to St. Paul, his hypothesis need not be considered as a purely naturalistic one.

(iii.) Chief of such naturalistic attempts is that which would represent the appearance as the result of St. Paul's psychological condition (Strauss, Baur, Holsten). Doubts or misgivings, so it is represented, had been working in his mind for some time previously, scruples of conscience as to his persecuting proceedings. Such scruples were induced largely by his experience of the calm confidence and triumphant joy of the Christians in persecution, as compared with his own inner consciousness of turmoil, born of the conflict between self and the holy law of God. Strauss's classical representation of the case may be quoted : " They [the believers in Jesus] showed a state of mind, a quiet peace, a tranquil cheerfulness, even under suffering, which put to shame the restless and joyless zeal of their persecutor. Could *he* have been a false teacher who had adherents such as these ? could that have been a mendacious pretence which gave such rest and security ? On the one hand, he saw the new sect in spite of all persecutions, nay, in consequence of them, extending their influence wider and wider around them ; on the other, as their persecutor he felt that inward tranquillity growing less and less which he could observe in so many ways in the persecuted. We cannot therefore be surprised if in hours of despondency and inward unhappiness he put to himself the question : ' Who after all is right, thou or the crucified Galilean about whom these men are so enthusiastic ?' And when he had once got as far as this the result, with his bodily and mental characteristics, naturally followed in an ecstasy in which the very same Christ whom to this time he had so passionately persecuted appeared to him in all the glory of which His adherents spoke so much, showed him the perversity and folly of his conduct, and called him to come over to His service" (*New Life of Jesus*, i. 420). Time and again—so C. Holsten represents the case in his searching analysis of St. Paul's state of mind at his conversion (*Zum Evangelium des Paulus und des Petrus*, Rostock, 1868)—the reproachful image of Jesus, as described by Stephen and other Christians, stood before his soul and made appeal so that he was half persuaded to join himself to His followers. In such a state of mind he journeyed to Damascus, when he experienced his vision. This view is supported, it is held, by the words reported in the narrative of his conversion as spoken to St. Paul by Christ Himself. "You hurt yourself by kicking at the goad" (Acts xxvi. 14). "In what else can it have consisted," asks Pfleiderer, "than in the painful doubt as to the lawfulness of his persecution of the Christians—in the doubt, therefore, whether the truth was really on his side, and not rather, after all, on that of the persecuted disciples of Christ ?" (*Influence of the Apostle Paul on the Development of Christianity* [*Hibbert Lects.*], Eng. tr., London, 1885, p. 35).

Now it is not necessary to deny all inward psychological preparation on St. Paul's side for the experience issuing in his conversion. Otherwise, as Pfleiderer truly enough observes, his conversion

would have to be regarded as a "magical act of God, in which the
soul of Paul would have succumbed to an alien force" (*ib.* p. 34).
"Such visions do not happen in a vacuum" (Moffatt, *Paul and
Paulinism*, London, 1910, p. 10; cf. P. Feine, *Theologie des Neuen
Testaments*, Leipzig, 1910, p. 202). It was the difference in this
inward or psychological preparation between Saul and his journey-
companions that partly explains why the occurrence meant one
thing to him and another to them.

As elements in Saul's psychological preparation contributing or
disposing towards the result, the two factors referred to by supporters
of this theory may be admitted. (1) The wonderful demeanour of
the followers of the crucified Nazarene, their triumphant joy and
calm, unswerving loyalty even in persecution, could not but leave a
powerful impression on such an ardent and sensitive nature as St
Paul's. In particular, the calm confidence and heroism of Stephen
in face of death and his dying vision of the Lord probably sank
deep into his soul. And then (2) the impression made by these
would be emphasized by contrast with his own experience of
inward turmoil and dispeace. The words reported in the narrative
of his conversion, "You hurt yourself by kicking at the goad"
($\sigma\kappa\lambda\eta\rho\delta\nu$ $\sigma o\iota$ $\pi\rho\delta\varsigma$ $\kappa\dot\epsilon\nu\tau\rho a$ $\lambda a\kappa\tau\dot\iota\zeta\epsilon\iota\nu$), are no doubt full of significance
in this connexion. Even if proverbial, and as such not to be
pressed too closely with regard to St. Paul's state of mind before
his conversion (so Knowling, in *Expos. Gk. Test.*, London, 1900, on
Acts xxvi. 14), taken in connexion with references in his letters they
reveal a profound internal conflict going on within Saul's soul, a
deep misgiving concerning his own religious position and standing
before God. A Pharisee of the Pharisees, he had striven to attain
peace with God through fulfilment of the Law, but already upon
him the painful sense of failure and moral despair was pressing (cf.
Rom. vii.). "His soul had been pierced and lacerated by his sense
of moral impotence in face of the Law. Like a stupid beast, Saul
knew not whither this incessant goad was driving him, nor whose
was the hand that plied it" (Findlay, Hastings' *Dict. of Bible*,
iii. 702[b]). He could not but contrast his own state of mind with
that of the followers of Jesus. But with all this there is in the
narratives no hint of doubt on Saul's part of the rectitude of his
persecuting zeal, nothing to show that he ever suspected the real
truth to lie in the direction of the new sect of the Nazarenes.

St. Paul's own uniform representation of his mental condition on
his way to Damascus is not that of doubtful misgiving, but of
conscious rectitude undisturbed by the least shadow of doubt that

in persecuting the Christians even to death, he was doing God's will. "I verily thought within myself that it was my duty to do many things contrary to the name of Jesus of Nazareth" (Acts xxvi. 9). To Saul the position of the Jesus-sect was a blasphemy against God. It was not only that their so-called Messiah had been put to death. That in itself to the mind of Saul, the orthodox Jew, shattered the claim that Jesus was the Christ. The conception of a Suffering Messiah was, to quote Holsten's own words, "so far removed from the orthodoxy of Jewish belief that a suffering Messiah, during the lifetime of Jesus, was still to His disciples an inconceivable and enigmatical representation" (*op. cit.* p. 98). But it was above all the peculiar form of the Death which disproved the claim of Jesus to be the Messiah. To a Jew, the Cross was the very emblem of Divine rejection. "Cursed," not merely by man but by God, "is everyone that hangeth on a tree" (Gal. iii. 13; cf. Deut. xxi. 23. Hence ἀνάθεμα Ἰησοῦς, 1 Cor. xii. 3). To the mind of Saul of Tarsus the death on the Cross appeared a Divine retribution on a blasphemous claim. God Himself had endorsed the verdict of Caiaphas and Pilate, and in proclaiming a crucified Messiah the followers of Jesus were fighting against God.

Thus to Saul the suppression of the Jesus-sect was a sacred duty and a meritorious service for the glory of God. The followers of Jesus spoke, indeed, of a resurrection of their crucified Master, but no one had seen Him save some of their own company, and to Saul's mind it was the uttermost heresy, and he simply refused to believe it. The young Pharisee was, indeed, far from being at peace within himself. Yet this very inward dispeace only fanned his anti-Christian zeal to new flame and urged him forward more fiercely than ever in loyal adherence to the traditions of his fathers, if thereby he might the better fulfil the righteousness of the Law. As he says himself, he was "exceedingly mad against them" (Acts xxvi. 11). With all the intensity of his nature he set himself to stamp out the heresy. Not content with harrying the Christians in Jerusalem, he "persecuted them even unto strange cities." Such was the spirit in which he started on his way to Damascus, when all at once his persecuting zeal was brought to a halt. An incident occurred which cleft his life in twain and "drove him, in spite of himself, into a new channel" (Sabatier, *The Apostle Paul*, p. 60). The mental conditions, therefore, out of which a self-generated vision of the Glorified Jesus might conceivably have been formed were wanting in him at the time.

The whole impression conveyed to the reader of the narrative in Acts is that of the suddenness, unexpectedness, surprisingness of the change in the persecutor's psychological condition (Acts ix. 3, xxii. 6). And this is corroborated by the references in St. Paul's own letters. He always referred to the event which formed the turning-point of his life as a sudden, surprising, overwhelming experience. The very language he uses in reference to it emphasizes this. "I was apprehended (κατελήφθην) by Christ Jesus" (Phil. iii. 12)—a remarkable word which denotes that the persecutor was seized upon suddenly, taken hold of by Christ, and subdued as if by main force. He looks upon himself in 2 Cor. ii. 14 as a suddenly subdued rebel, whom God leads in triumph about the world. The same suggestion of suddenness and violence we have seen already to be implied in the term ἔκτρωμα. That this, and not a gradual change, is the view required by St. Paul's language is admitted by so unprejudiced a critic as H. J. Holtzmann in his edition of the *Acts*: "It is at all events certain that the Apostle knows nothing of a gradual process which has drawn him closer to Christianity, but only of a sudden halt which he was compelled to make in the midst of an active career" (*Handkommentar zum Neuen Testament*[3], Tübingen, 1901, ii. 70 f., quoted by Knowling, *Testimony of St. Paul*, p. 189).

CHAPTER IV

THE APOSTOLIC EVIDENCE FOR THE FACT OF THE RESURRECTION (*Continued*)

II. THE DOCUMENTARY EVIDENCE (*Continued*)

2. THE WITNESS OF THE GOSPELS

THE apostles, in their preaching of Jesus and the Resurrection, would from the first be called upon to substantiate their statements by detailed historical evidence. One of the first requirements in missionary teaching of the Resurrection would be a summary of the principal witnesses. Thus arose, we may well believe, for missionary and catechetical purposes such a list of the chief Appearings as that given in 1 Cor. xv. 3–8. But, especially as time went on, more would be required than this. "How can you believe in a crucified Messiah?" "How can you preach the gospel of forgiveness and justification in His name?" To such challenging questions the full answer would be not merely an adducing of the evidence for the Resurrection, but an account of the life and ministry of Jesus on earth —essentially a *Passions-Geschichte*—showing that the suffering of the Death was the climax of a life of service and sacrifice on the part of One who claimed to be the

Messiah, and who supported His claim by His works. So the main facts of Christ's life and teaching on earth would be recalled, and an oral tradition would grow up based on first-hand evidence derived from the apostles and other eye-witnesses; until, as time went on and the possibility of distorting the fact grew ever greater, it would become necessary for apologetic and practical purposes to put on record the tradition hitherto preserved in the Church only by oral means. Thus arose written narratives of our Lord's life and ministry as culminating in the Death and Resurrection, the primary aim of which was not historical or biographical, but that expressed by the word "gospel." "These signs are recorded that you may believe that Jesus is the Christ, the Son of God; and that believing you may have life through his name" (John xx. 31; cf. Mark's heading of his work, "The beginning of the gospel of Jesus Christ, the Son of God," i. 1).

The generally accepted results of recent criticism with regard to the relations of the Gospels may be represented shortly as follows. Two main sources are to be recognized : (1) a collection made at a fairly early date of the sayings and discourses of Jesus, the chief object of which was, according to Sanday, "to set before its readers (the new converts in the different Churches) some account of the Christian ideal, the character and mode of life expected of them as Christians" (*Encycl. of Religion and Ethics*, ii. 575ª). This original document is identified with the *Logia* mentioned by Papias (Eus. *Eccles. Hist.*, iii. 39) and usually christened "Q" (*Quelle*, the original source). (2) A later document supplementing Q, a narrative or sketch of the Lord's public ministry which was practically, if not quite, identical with our present Second Gospel written by John Mark, the companion of Peter, and embodying the substance of that apostle's reminiscences of his Master's words and works. (The original ending of the narrative is lost, and the present ending (xvi. 9–20) is a later appendix; but the fact that it appears in

nearly all extant MSS. and versions points to an early date, and perhaps
to a close relation with Mark himself.)   Then a little later came
two fuller narratives, going behind the Ministry to the Birth.   The
writers, Matthew and Luke, writing for different classes of readers,
with the two main sources referred to before them as basis of their
narratives, arranged and edited independently the material thus
supplied, sometimes interpreting it, sometimes giving it new point
and fullness, and each adding information derived from his own
minute investigations.   This dependence of Matthew and Luke in
their narrative portions on Mark is reckoned "the one solid contribution" of literary criticism (F. C. Burkitt, *The Gospel History
and its Transmission*, Edinburgh, 1906, p. 37 ; cf. W. C. Allen,
Internat. Crit. Comm., " S. Matthew "[3], do., 1912, p. vii).

It cannot, however, be argued that, while Mark is a primary
authority, Matthew and Luke are secondary authorities.   Much
critical argument proceeds on this assumption, as if the narratives
of the First and Third Gospels were a simple "writing up" and
embellishing of Mark's stories, and any details not found in the
latter were to be rejected as unhistorical and legendary.   Luke, *e.g.*,
in the most important portion of his whole narrative—the Passion
and the Resurrection sections—wholly deserts Mark and prefers to
rely on independent information.   As to the source of this information, Chase (*Gospels in the Light of Hist. Criticism*, pp. 12, 62 f.)
makes out a strong case for James and the elders of the Church
with whom Luke was brought into personal contact in Jerusalem
some twenty-five years after the Passion (see Acts xxi. 15 ff.).   Now
James was a primary witness of the Resurrection, one of those who
saw the Lord, so that Luke in his narrative would be in touch with
first-hand information as much as Mark (cf. Luke i. 2).   Then
later still, the writer of the Fourth Gospel, having a knowledge of
the Synoptic Gospels, wrote his narrative, wishing to supplement
and perhaps in some details to correct them.   In connexion with
the narrative of the Resurrection in particular, the writer, with his
more precise and consecutive account, affords valuable information.
There is a growing tendency among critics to hold that, in substance
at least, this Gospel represents or is based on authentic historical
reminiscences of the Lord's words and works from the pen or lips of
the apostle John in his old age.   These reminiscences indeed have
been moulded by the writer's meditation through many years on
their significance, so that reminiscence and interpretation are often
so interwoven that it is difficult to say where one ends and the
other begins, but this does not detract from the trustworthy

4

character of the Gospel. "It is a blending of fact and interpretation; but the interpretation comes from one who had an unique position and unique advantages for getting at the heart and truth of that which he sought to interpret. It is the mind of Christ seen through the medium of one of the first and closest of His companions" (Sanday, *The Criticism of the Fourth Gospel*, Oxford, 1905, p. 169). Indeed, John's account may be truest to reality. "The history of a great movement will be told long years afterwards with the nearest approach to truth, not by the prosaic observer who noticed only what lay on the surface, but rather by one who at the time discerned something of its grandeur, and who as he recalled it instinctively idealized it. Idealization is perhaps a necessary condition for the preservation of the memory of a momentary spiritual crisis" (Chase, p. 17). (Chap. xxi. is an appendix to the Gospel which closed at the end of chap. 20. Yet it must have become an integral part of the Gospel at an early period, for no trace exists of a Gospel without it. The style also is similar to the rest of the Gospel, so that on both internal and external evidence an increasing number of critics support Godet's contention : "Either John himself composed this piece some time after having finished the Gospel, or we have here the work of that circle of friends and disciples who surrounded the apostle at Ephesus, who had often heard him relate the facts contained in it, and who have reproduced them in his own language.")

It is often urged against the narratives of the Gospels that none of the writers were first-hand witnesses, but if the Fourth Gospel, as a growing weight of criticism encourages us to believe, represents authentic reminiscences of the apostle John, we have at least one such witness of first-rank importance. But further, Mark was the companion and interpreter of Peter, another primary witness. Besides, Luke was the companion of St. Paul, and St. Paul had direct communication with Peter, James, and other members of the original apostolic company ; and Luke lays stress on the fact that the things which he relates rested on the testimony of those who were eye-witnesses. The Gospel of Matthew, if not directly the work of that apostle—another first-hand witness—must have been written by one so closely associated with him that it ever afterwards passed as Matthew's own. We are thus, throughout, in contact with first-hand information, and all claim to be but recording a tradition well established in the Church, and derived originally from the apostles.

Approximate probable dates for the Gospels may be given as follows: Mark A.D. 65–70, Matt. Luke (Gospel and Acts) A.D. 70–85,

John A.D. 90–100—all falling probably within the first century The extra-canonical Gospels, the *Gospel according to the Hebrews* and the *Gospel of Peter*, parts of which have been preserved, and both of which belong probably to the beginning of the second century, add little or nothing of a trustworthy character to the canonical accounts of the Resurrection.

The witness to the Resurrection in the Gospels may be thus exhibited :

(*a*) Empty grave on the third day (Mark xv. 42–xvi. 8 ; Matt. xxvii. 57–xxviii. 8 ; Luke xxiii. 50–xxiv. 12 (22–24) ; John xix. 38–xx. 13).

And (*b*) post-Resurrection appearings (Mark [App.] xvi. 9–20 ; Matt. xxviii. 9–20 ; Luke xxiv. 12–53 ; John xx. 14–29, xxi. [App.] ; *Gospel acc. to Hebrews*, xii. 50–57, *Gospel of Peter*, xiv. 58–60).

The historical value of the Gospel witness to the Resurrection has been called in question on various grounds, chief of which are : (1) Alleged discrepancies between the different accounts. This was already one of the chief objections to the Gospels in the earliest reasoned criticism of Christianity that has come down to us—*The True Word* of Celsus, written about the end of the second century (see Origen, *c. Celsum*, ii. 56–63, v. 56, 58). H. S. Reimarus, writing nearly a century and a half ago, enumerated ten irreconcilable contradictions or discrepancies in the narratives (G. E. Lessing, *Wolfenbütteler Fragmente*, 1774–78). "In reality," says a more recent critic, "the number is much greater" (Schmiedel, *Encycl. Bibl.* iv. 4041). And Harnack, on the basis of examination of the various narratives, feels himself driven to an agnostic despair of history, which regards the problem of what happened on the first

Easter morning as absolutely insoluble. (2) The presence of mythical and legendary elements in the accounts. "Even the empty grave on the third day can by no means be regarded as a certain historical fact, because it appears united in the accounts with manifest legendary features" (Harnack, *Hist. of Dogma*, Eng. tr., 7 vols., London, 1894–99, i. 85 n.). (3) The insufficiency of the evidence, even if allowed, to satisfy the demands of scientific historical inquiry. "Secure evidence of the resurrection of Jesus would be the attestation of it in a decided and accordant manner by impartial witnesses. But . . . Jesus showed himself to his adherents only : why not also to his enemies, that they too might be convinced, and that by their testimony posterity might be precluded from every conjecture of a designed fraud on the part of his disciples?" (Strauss, *Life of Jesus*, Eng. tr.[2], London, 1892, pt. iii. ch. iv. sect. 140, p. 738). To like purpose Renan demands that the evidence for the Resurrection be such as would convince "a commission, composed of physiologists, physicists, chemists, persons accustomed to historical criticism," and on this basis criticizes the New Testament narratives as not satisfying "scientific conditions" or "rational principles" (*Life of Jesus*, Eng. tr., London, 1873, Introd., p. 29 f.). We shall consider the two parts of the witness separately, keeping these objections in view.

(a) *The Empty Grave*

The narratives agree as to the following facts : (1) On the morning of the first day of the week, "the third

day" after the Crucifixion, very early, certain women
went to the grave (Matt. xxviii. 1 ; Mark xvi. 1 f. ;
Luke xxiv. 1, 10 ; John xx. 1) ; (2) they found the
stone rolled away and the grave empty (Matt. xxviii.
2–7 ; Mark xvi. 3–6 ; Luke xxiv. 2–6 ; John xx. 1, 11 f.) ;[1]
(3) they were informed by angelic means that Jesus
had risen, and that they were bidden to convey the
news to the disciples (Matt. xxviii. 5–8 ; Mark xvi. 6–8 ;
Luke xxiv. 4–11 ; John xx. 11 f.). Divergences in
detail have to be acknowledged, though they are slight
in comparison with the general agreement, and do not
impugn the trustworthiness of the central facts in the
common tradition.

Chief of these divergences are the following : (1) In regard to
the number of the women, John represents the visit to the
sepulchre as made by Mary Magdalene alone (xx. 1), while the
others (Matthew, Mark, Luke) represent her as in company with
other women, variously named. (2) As regards the purpose attri-
buted to the women in coming to the tomb, two of the Evangelists,
Mark (xvi. 1) and Luke (xxiii. 56, xxiv. 1), represent this purpose
as the anointing of the body of Jesus, while John records the fact
that the anointing had already been done by Joseph and Nicodemus
at the time of the entombment. (3) In regard to the angelic
message, Matthew and Mark speak of one angel at the tomb ;
Mark representing him as "a young man" arrayed in a white
robe, appearing to the women on their "entering into the tomb"
(xvi. 15), while Matthew has an independent story of a great
earthquake, and represents the angel as rolling away the stone and
sitting upon it (*i.e.* outside the tomb, xxviii. 2–5). Luke and John,
on the other hand, speak of two angels as appearing to the women
(or woman), Luke representing the interview as occurring inside

---

[1] It should be noted that, though we speak, following Scripture
usage, of the empty grave "on the third day," the body of Jesus lay
in the grave only one whole day and a few hours of other two—
probably less than a day and a half in all.

the tomb (xxiv. 3–5), while John represents Mary Magdalene as still remaining outside (xx. 12).

In regard to such divergences or alleged "discrepancies" we have to remember two things. (1) The aim of the narratives is not to supply evidence or proof for a court of law, but rather to supply information regarding facts already believed, as Luke says, "fully established" ($\pi\epsilon\pi\lambda\eta\rho o\phi o\rho\eta\mu\acute{\epsilon}\nu\omega\nu$), in the Church, concerning which they had already been "catechetically instructed" (ver. 4, $\kappa\alpha\tau\eta\chi\acute{\eta}\theta\eta s$). This explains the often naive and informal character of the narratives. None of the Evangelists aims at giving a complete account of everything that happened on that wonderful Easter morning and day. Each selects and combines with his own special object in view. From this incompleteness arises much of the seeming contradictoriness of the different narratives. *E.g.*, John speaks only of Mary Magdalene at the sepulchre, probably because he has a special story to tell of her —though the "we" of John xx. 2 seems to imply the presence of others. (There is no need to suppose that the women came all together to the sepulchre. It is more probable that they came in different groups or companies.) (2) We have to remember further that the Resurrection day was necessarily one of intense excitement and agitation. This is vividly reflected in the narratives—the shock of amazement of the witnesses, their incredulity, their mingled fear and joy. So it is possible that the events of the day were told by different witnesses in a different order, and with differences in detail. The excitement of the moment may have left the memory dazed and unable to form any distinct impression of what was seen and heard, so that from the first there would be a certain confusion in the stories. But to discredit the narratives because they betray imperfections such as these is altogether unreasonable. So far from being incompatible with, they rather confirm, their historical veracity. "The usual character of human testimony is substantial truth under circumstantial variety" (W. Paley, *Evidences of Christianity*, in J. S. Memes' *Christian Evidences*, London, 1859, pt. iii. ch. i. p. 203).

It need not be denied that some details of the narratives may possibly be unhistorical or legendary. In Matthew's story, *e.g.*, about the resurrection of many bodies of the saints, and their appearance to many after the Resurrection (xxvii. 51 f.), we seem to have some-

thing akin to what we find in the Apocryphal Gospels
(cf. Chase, *Gospels in the Light of Hist. Criticism*, p. 31).
But the earthquake account (given only by Matthew,
which is the only account of how the stone was rolled
away) and that of the angelic visitation when ruled out
as legendary and unhistorical (*e.g.* Lake, *Resurrection*,
p. 251 f.), are so not so much because of any insufficiency
of evidence, as through prejudice against the supernatural, which, however, is of the very essence of the
narratives throughout.

Luke records (xxiv. 12) that, on receipt of the
message of the women, Peter went to the sepulchre and
found it empty, with only the grave-clothes left. This
verse is of doubtful authority — being absent from
important Western documents — and is omitted by
Westcott and Hort and by Tischendorf as a later
insertion, though, as F. Blass points out (*Philology of
the Gospels*, London, 1898, p. 189), Luke's account
contains another reference to a visit to the grave on the
part of some of the apostles (ver. 24), the genuineness of
which there is no good ground for calling in question.

John in his account—that of an eye-witness of the
facts—tells us (xx. 3–10) that, on receipt of the
message of the women, Peter and himself went to the
grave and found the condition as the women had said.
He gives a circumstantial description of the way in
which the grave-clothes were found lying; in particular,
that the napkin which had been round His head was
found " folded up " (ver. 7, ἐντετυλιγμένον) by itself, apart
from the other bandages, doubtless at the raised end of
the chamber where the head rested (see Latham, *Risen*

Master, plate 2, for an imaginary sketch of the interior of the tomb). Latham's theory is that the word implies that the head-cloth still partially retained its annular form (p. 43), and that the other grave-clothes still retained the general outline of the human form (p. 50). If this interpretation be correct, the suggestion of the careful observer (θεωρεῖ, John xx. 6) would be that the Body had somehow passed out of the grave-clothes, rather than that it had been removed by human hands for burial elsewhere. In any case, the position of the clothes is noted by the Evangelist as significant.

In this connexion the significance of the incident recorded in Matt. xxviii. 11–15 is to be noted—the attempt of the Jewish authorities to bribe the guard to misrepresent the facts and say that the disciples removed the body—a saying which is "commonly reported among the Jews until this day." This fraudulent transaction proceeds upon the admission by the enemies of Christianity that the grave was empty— an admission which is enough to show that the evidence for the empty grave was "too notorious to be denied" (*Cambridge Theological Essays*, ed. H. B. Swete, London, 1905, p. 336).

The whole story of the guard at the tomb, which is narrated only by Matthew (xxvii. 62–66) has been called in question. But the action of the authorities in setting a watch at the tomb is altogether credible. Had not Jesus spoken repeatedly of His being put to death and rising again the third day (Matt. xvi. 21, xvii. 22 f., xx. 16, 19, and parallels)? And may not such words have come to the ears of His enemies? Had not indeed His mysterious words about the building of the Temple in three days been quoted against Him before the chief priests and Pharisees (Mark xiv. 58; cf. John ii. 18–22)? And with such in their minds, was not the fact that the body of Jesus had been committed to His friends for burial enough to create the fear that His disciples might remove it and afterwards pretend that He had risen? To meet this apprehension, a watch was obtained, and to make security doubly sure, the tomb was sealed with the official seal.

Nothing, indeed, in the Resurrection-story of the narratives is more strongly attested than the fact of the empty tomb on the third day after the Crucifixion. It is not only attested by the women, and subsequently by Peter and John — "interested parties" — but also acknowledged by foes. This is the fundamental fact at the basis of the apostolic belief in the Resurrection on the third day. It is not uncommon among negative critics to represent the case as if the belief were a deduction of inference from certain prophetic references, a belief resting "on theological rather than historical grounds" (Lake, *Resurrection of Jesus Christ*, p. 264). Strauss set the way in his endeavour to show how the belief might have originated from Old Testament hints (*New Life of Jesus*, i. 438 f.). O. Holtzmann (*Life of Jesus*, Eng. tr., London, 1904, p. 336) lays much stress on Hos. vi. 2: "After two days will he revive us: on the third day he will raise us up, and we shall live before him." Schmiedel (*Encycl. Bibl.* iv. 4067) appeals to 2 Kings xx. 5 as a text that has "special relevance" in this connexion. Others combine with these Old Testament hints the predictions of Jesus Himself (*e.g.* Meyer, *Die Auferstehung Christi*, p. 181 f.), while more recently others trace the belief primarily to a "Messianic dogmatic," a pre-Christian sketch of a dying and rising Messiah which found its way into Jewish writings from Oriental sources, chiefly Babylonian (see, *e.g.*, Lake, pp.

197 f., 261 ; Cheyne, *Bible Problems*, p. 110 ff.).   The Old
Testament hints and pre-Christian Messianic belief alone
or combined with the predictions of Jesus, it is represented, naturally took shape in the belief in the
Resurrection on the third day, or were the predisposing
cause for this belief.   The belief created the Resurrection
rather than the Resurrection the belief.   But what are
the facts ?   The Gospels tell us unmistakably that the
disciples had no anticipation whatever of the resurrection of their crucified Master.   For all that Jesus did
predict His resurrection on the third day and represent
this as foreshadowed in the Scriptures (Matt. xvi. 21,
xvii. 22 f., xx. 16, 19 ; Mark viii. 31, ix. 31, x. 33 ;
Luke ix. 22, xviii. 31, xxiv. 6, 7 ; cf. Luke xxiv. 46),
the astonishment of the disciples at the empty tomb is
explained by the reflexion that " as yet they knew not
the scripture, that he must rise again from the dead "
(John xx. 9).   So far from the victory of the Messiah
over death through a resurrection being part of the
current Jewish Messianic belief, the very idea of a
suffering and dying Messiah was, as Holsten acknowledges,
" to His disciples an inconceivable and enigmatical representation " (*op. cit.* p. 98 ; cf. Matt. xvi. 21, xvii. 23).
" Suffering and death for the actual possessor of the
Messianic dignity are in fact unimaginable, according to
the testimony of the prophets " (Dalman, *Words of Jesus*,
Eng. tr., Edinburgh, 1902, p. 265).   Ps. xvi. 10 is the
only passage which the New Testament writers quote as
prophetic of the Resurrection, but it is clear that its
Christian interpretation was by no means obvious *before*
the event.   The proof from Scripture prophecy of the

Resurrection on the third day was thus an interpretation or confirmation *after* the event, and, under the influence of Jesus' post-Resurrection teaching, an " afterthought," as Lake himself admits (p. 30). It is not the prophecies which suggest the fact, but the fact which extracts and explains the prophecies. The attempt to trace the belief in the event " on the third day " ultimately to Oriental sources will be more fully considered below (p. 183 ff.). But meantime the fact is to be emphasized that no detail is better attested in connexion with the Resurrection than the discovery of the empty tomb on the third day, and any criticism which ignores this cannot justly lay claim to be " scientific " (cf. Lagrange, *St. Marc*, Paris, 1911, p. 415 ff.).

It has often been pointed out that in the Gospels none of the witnesses claims to have seen our Lord leave the tomb. Of the Resurrection itself there was no eye-witness. This is sometimes adduced in disparagement of the Gospel evidence. But this very silence of the narratives is a significant corroboration of their historical trustworthiness. If the accounts of the events at the empty grave were as legendary as some recent criticism would represent, the silence is almost inexplicable. " A faith that was capable of creating, with absolutely no basis in fact, so circumstantial an account of the emptiness of the Tomb, would assuredly not have left without a witness the one moment on which the significance of its whole creation seems to depend " (*Cambridge Theol. Essays*, p. 332). A comparison with the account given in the apocryphal *Gospel of Peter* brings into clear relief the self-restraint of the canonical Gospels (cf. Orr, *Resurrection of Jesus*, p. 260 f.).

(b) *The post-Resurrection Appearings*

Though the empty grave on the third day is thus adequately attested, this, according to the evidence, was not in and by itself the cause of the disciples' belief in the

Resurrection.   According to the Evangelists, it was not simply the fact of the empty tomb, not even this supplemented by the angelic proclamation that the Lord had risen, which produced in the disciples the conviction that their crucified Master was indeed risen from the dead. The women returned, as they were bidden, to tell the disciples what they had seen and heard at the empty grave, but "this story of the women seemed in their opinion to be nonsense (λῆρος); they would not believe them" (Luke xxiv. 11 [Moffatt]; cf. Mark xvi. 11, 13, 14; John xx. 25, οὐ μὴ πιστεύσω.   For a whole week Thomas refused to believe).   Peter and John go to the grave and find the condition of things as the women had said.   They stoop down and enter in and find the grave-clothes lying where the body had rested, with the head-cloth folded up by itself, instead of lying beside the other bandages, and they return home "wondering what had happened" (Luke xxiv. 12 [Moffatt]), perplexed and unable to explain what they saw.   John indeed, writing many years after, says of himself that he "saw and believed" (John xx. 8, εἶδε καὶ ἐπίστευσεν).   The meaning of these words is doubtful.   It has been suggested that, from the manner in which the grave-clothes lay folded, John was led not merely to belief in the emptiness of the grave, but to the idea of resurrection.   So, *e.g.*, Cyril of Alexandria: "Ex involutis linteaminibus resurrectionem colligunt," as the Latin version renders it (Migne, vii. 683, quoted by W. J. S. Simpson in *Dict. of Christ and Gospels*, ii. 507[a]); cf. Latham, *Risen Master*, and Dods, *Expos. Gk. Test.*, *in loc.* But if such was the case, it does not appear that he said anything to the others on the subject. On the other hand, to say that "believed" here means simply that he "became convinced" that the grave was empty and the body removed may be saying too little. Probably it is nearest the truth to say with Swete: "There arose in his [John's] mind at that moment a nascent confidence that in some way as yet unknown their darkness would be turned to light, and the victory of the Christ be secured. For the present, however, the mystery remained unsolved; they seemed to have exhausted their means of getting at the truth, and both men went home again" (*Appearances*, p. 6). Even as regards the women themselves, the chief impression we receive of their mental condition from the narratives is that of terrorized amazement. The dazzling vision and the voice from the grave filled them with dismay. They fled from the sepulchre, and on their way back to the city they spoke not a word, so great was their terror. "They were seized with terror and beside themselves" (Mark xvi. 8 [Moffatt]). Not the empty grave, therefore, and not the angelic report merely, but these followed by and in essential connexion with the subsequent self-revelation of the risen living Lord in the shape of manifestations or appearings of Himself to them (or what were taken to be such), were what, according to the narratives, gave rise to the apostles' belief in the Resurrection.

The list of the Appearings given in the various narratives is as follows:

(1) *Mark's* account (in the genuine portion) records none. But the abrupt way in which the narrative

breaks off in the middle of a sentence at xvi. 8 ("for they were afraid of . . ." [Moffatt]) points to the fact that the writer meant to add some account of the meeting of the Risen Lord with the disciples in Galilee referred to in ver. 7. The probability is that such was added and that it is lost. There is good reason for believing that Matthew has worked up into his last chapter much of the matter contained in the lost ending of Mark, adding certain incidents for which he relied upon his own resources (see Chase's art. "The Lord's Command to Baptize" in *Journal of Theol. Studies*, vi. [1904–05] 481 ff.). The Mark App. (xvi. 9–20) records Appearings to Mary Magdalene (ver. 9), to two disciples on the way to Emmaus (ver. 12), and to the Eleven at meat (ver. 14).

(2) *Matthew* records two Appearings : the first to the women in or near Jerusalem on the morning of the Resurrection (xxviii. 9 f.), and then to the Eleven in Galilee on a mountain "where Jesus had appointed them" (vers. 16–20), the meeting referred to in forecast in Mark.

(3) *Luke* records three : to the two disciples on the way to Emmaus (xxiv. 13–32), to the "eleven . . . and them that were with them" in Jerusalem (ver. 36 ff.), and to Peter, this preceding the last and being indirectly stated (ver. 34 ; cf. 1 Cor. xv. 5). Luke also refers (ver. 50 f.) to a meeting on the day of Ascension at Bethany (more fully reported in Acts i. 4–12).

(4) *John*, writing with knowledge of the other Gospels and filling up from his reminiscences what the others had left untold, records four : an Appearing to Mary Magdalene in the garden (xx. 14–17); one to

the disciples (without Thomas) the same evening in Jerusalem (vers. 19–25); another a week later to the disciples (with Thomas) in Jerusalem (vers. 26–28); and, lastly, an Appearing to seven disciples some time later at the Sea of Tiberias (xxi. 1–14).

(5) *Extra-canonical Gospels.*—The *Gospel according to the Hebrews* tells of an Appearing to James, and the *Gospel of Peter* seems on the point of narrating an incident not unlike the appearance to the seven at the Sea of Tiberias when the fragment ends abruptly. Both narratives, however, are distinctly secondary in character and add nothing of a trustworthy nature to the canonical accounts.

It is against the accounts of the Appearings in the Gospels that the argument from discrepancies has most force. It has to be frankly admitted that the records present many difficulties in the way of constructing a coherent harmonized account. "Whichever way we turn, difficulties meet us, which the documents to which we have access do not enable us to remove" (Sanday, *Outlines of Life of Christ,* p. 180). These difficulties concern in the main two points: (i.) the sequence or time order of the Appearings, and (ii.) their place or locality.

(i.) *The sequence or time order of the Appearings.*— None of the Gospels presents us with an ordered statement of the whole facts. St. Paul's list in 1 Cor. xv. is no doubt given in chronological order, but it does not profess to be complete, and leaves room for other Appearings to be added. By the time the Gospel accounts were written, however, it may have been too late to find out with any precision how this or that additional Appearing preserved in tradition was related in time to

the others.   In particular the relation of the Appearing
to Mary Magdalene (recorded by John and Mark
App.) to the Appearing to the women recorded in
Matt. xxviii. 9–10 is left by the narratives in uncertainty
—an uncertainty connected with the seeming confusion
in the First and Third Gospels between Mary's return
to Jerusalem and the return of the other women.   Again,
Luke gives the impression that all the Appearings took
place on the day of the Resurrection, and that the
Ascension itself took place on the evening of that day.
But this is contrary to what we find in the other
Gospel accounts, where the Appearings are represented as
extending over a considerable time.   And it is contrary
to Luke's own account in Acts i., where he interposes
" forty days " between the Resurrection and the Ascension,
and assumes the appearings of Christ to be spread over
the whole period (cf. Acts xiii. 31, " many days ").   The
latter " contradiction " is made much of by Strauss and
Keim, and, more recently, by Weizsäcker and Meyer.
The explanation is to be found, however, in Luke's highly
compressed or condensed style of narrative in the closing
chapter of his Gospel (cf. Ramsay, *St. Paul the Traveller
and the Roman Citizen*, London, 1895, p. 17, " compressed
to the highest degree ").   Chase maintains that there
are good grounds for thinking that the opening section
of the Acts was already composed before the closing
section of the Gospel (*Gospels*, p. 46), and Denney says
that in all probability it was produced continuously with
it (*Jesus and the Gospel*, p. 142).   Having in view from
the beginning to write a sequel to his Gospel, giving a
more detailed account of the events leading up to the

Ascension, the Evangelist " fore-shortens " and compresses
the narrative in the Gospel, treating two or three distinct
occasions as if they were continuous, knowing that facts
well known in the Church would render impossible the
supposition that all the events recorded took place in a
single day.

(ii.) *The scene or locality of the Appearings.*—More
serious is the difficulty which confronts us here. St.
Paul in 1 Cor. xv. makes no mention of locality, but the
Gospel accounts are divided between Galilee and Jerusalem. Matthew and probably Mark (original conclusion) lay the stress upon Galilee. In Mark indeed (in
the genuine portion) no record is given of any Appearings, but the women are bidden by the angel at the tomb
to say that the Risen Lord would meet the disciples in
Galilee (xvi. 7). The same message of the angel is given
even more emphatically in Matt. xxviii. 7—" Go quickly
and tell "—and (unless vers. 9–10 represent, as P.
Rohrbach maintains [see A. B. Bruce, *Expos. Gk. Test.*, *in
loc.*], the same fact in another form) repeated by Jesus
Himself when He appears to these women on their way
to execute the charge of the angel (xxviii. 10). A
promise to the same effect had already been given by
Jesus to His disciples before they left the upper room
for the Garden of Gethsemane, and is recorded by both
Matthew and Mark (Matt. xxvi. 32 ; Mark xiv. 28).

In accordance with this message and promise is the
programme of Appearings given in the First Gospel.
The eleven disciples departed into Galilee (xxviii. 16),
and there saw Jesus, and there also received the great
commission, Go and make disciples of all nations. No

record is given of any appearing of Jesus to the apostles in or near Jerusalem. And it is probable that the original conclusion of Mark carried out the same programme. Luke and John, however, confine their account to Appearings in Jerusalem and neighbourhood. Luke, who records (in chap. xxiv.) the appearances to the two on the way to Emmaus, to Peter, and to the Eleven, all in or near Jerusalem, ends his account with a command of Jesus to the disciples to remain in Jerusalem until they were "clothed with power from on high" (ver. 49). But this seems definitely to exclude any departure into Galilee, and the possibility of an appearance there. In line with this is the different representation of the angelic message given in Luke from that in Matthew and Mark. The Marcan version, "He goeth before you into Galilee: there shall ye see him, as he said unto you" (xvi. 7), becomes in Luke, "Remember how he spake unto you when he was yet in Galilee, saying," etc. (xxiv. 6 f.). That is to say, the message as given by Luke becomes not a direction to go into Galilee, but a reminder that Christ spoke to them about His resurrection when He was yet with them in Galilee. In like manner, all the Appearings mentioned in the Fourth Gospel except that in the Appendix (chap. xxi.) are placed in Jerusalem, and the author indicates that the disciples remained at least a week in Jerusalem after the Resurrection (xx. 26).

What are we to make of this discrepancy? Are these two versions or traditions to be regarded as contradictory and "irreconcilable" alternatives, only one of which can be received, the other being ruled out as unhistorical? This is how e.g., Strauss and Weizsäcker represent the case (*New Life of Jesus*, i. 435, and *Apost. Age*², i. 2 f.). If so, the question is, Which is the more trustworthy ? The usual course among critics has been to prefer the tradition in Matthew and Mark as the more primary, and to confine the Appearings to Galilee. The Appearings to the apostles at Jerusalem were, it is represented, unknown to Matthew and Mark, and form a later addition to the earliest version of the Resurrection-story which spoke only of Galilee.

This Galilæan theory, which we shall go on to discuss, is generally maintained in connexion with a naturalistic visionary theory of the Resurrection. The advantage of it for this purpose is obvious. By separating the appearances from the events of the third day and trans-ferring them to Galilee, it gives more time for visions to develop amid scenes coloured by memory and imagina-tion. As Strauss puts it, " If the transference of the appearances to Galilee dis-engages us from the third day as the period of the commencement of them, the longer time thus gained makes the reaction in the minds of the disciples more conceivable " (*New Life*, i. 437). Support for this Galilæan theory has been sought in the extra-canonical *Gospel of Peter*, where in xiv. 58–60 the dis-ciples are represented as returning to Galilee in sorrow and therefore without knowledge of the Resurrection. The difficulties of this theory have been forcibly pointed out by F. Loofs (*Die Auferstehungsberichte und ihr Wert*, Leipzig, 1898, pp. 18–25), who shows that it requires an impossible misrepresentation of the facts. To place the first appearance of our Lord in Galilee, it is of course necessary to transfer the apostles from Jerusalem.   But this has no historical basis whatever.   The words, "they [the disciples] all forsook him and fled" (Mark xiv. 50), the upholders of this theory interpret as referring to a flight not from the Garden of Gethsemane, but direct home to Galilee.

This interpretation, however, is refuted by the facts recorded.   It is, as J. Weiss calls it, "a scientific legend."   The oldest tradition expressly mentions that on the very night of the flight Peter was found in the high priest's palace (Mark xiv. 54 ; cf. Matt. xxvi. 5–8) and there thrice denied his Lord.   The message sent to the disciples through the women on Easter Day, according to the earliest Evangelist, was this, "He goeth *before* you into Galilee," implying, as Loofs points out (p. 19), that the disciples were still waiting in Jerusalem.   And so John, who predicts the "scattering" (xvi. 32), yet gives detailed accounts of the meetings in Jerusalem. If Matt. xxviii. 9–10 is accepted as genuine, the fact that the Evangelist records the Appearing to the women in Jerusalem, in which the previous direction of the angels to the disciples to go into Galilee is received from Jesus' own lips, shows that the appointed meeting in Galilee was not held to exclude earlier Appearings.

Further (see Chase, *Gospels*, p. 45), to argue that the silence of Matthew (probably following his source Mark) as to any Appearing to the apostles in Jerusalem, means ignorance of the fact, and that, therefore, the Appearings in or near Jerusalem are to be looked upon as a later addition to the earliest form of the Resurrection-story, which spoke only of Galilee, proves too much. Even as regards Galilee, Matthew mentions only one

Appearing to the Apostles. Are we, therefore, to conclude that he and his "source" were unaware of any other Appearing? We know from St. Paul that a list of Appearings was handed down in the Apostolic Church from the earliest times, and that this formed part of the catechetical instruction given in the churches. The facts about the Appearings, therefore, would be familiar to his readers, and just here may be found the sufficient explanation of their silence. The Evangelists felt at liberty to make a selection of the facts, each from his own point of view.

If the theory which would confine all the Appearings to Galilee is thus unsuccessful in accounting for the facts, is Loofs any more successful in transferring all the Appearings to Jerusalem, as he does in arguing in favour of the tradition represented by Luke and John? To carry out his theory, Loofs is obliged to separate John xxi. from the rest of the Gospel, treating it as having little or no connexion with it, and finding in it a combination of two incidents, one of which (the fishing scene of vers. 1–14) has been misplaced (Luke v. 1–11), while the other (the dialogue of vers. 15–23) was originally unconnected with Galilee. On this, suffice it to quote what Sanday says : " These are strong measures, which, however high our estimate of the tradition, Luke–John, are obviously not open to one who thinks that the identity of style between John xxi. and the rest of the Gospel is too great to permit of their separation " (Hastings' *Dict. of Bible*, ii. 640[b]).

The attempt to treat the narratives as alternatives and to confine the appearances either to Galilee or to

Jerusalem being thus unsatisfactory, we seem compelled to combine the traditions much as they are combined in the Fourth Gospel (with App.) and in the App. to Mark, and to recognize Appearings both in Jerusalem and in Galilee. If Matt. xxviii. 9–10 is to be treated as a later addition, the purpose of the insertion apparently, as Rohrbach suggests, was to cancel the impression otherwise produced that Jesus was seen only in Galilee. This is supported by St. Paul's list of Appearings in 1 Cor. xv. which, though it makes no mention of place, " suggests Galilee for the scene of the appearance to the 500 hardly less clearly than it suggests Jerusalem for the appearance to Peter and the Eleven."

We cannot, indeed, fit the narratives into each other so as to leave no difficulties or contradictions unsolved. The records are fragmentary, and as regards the details of the different traditions it would seem that from the first there was a certain amount of confusion which was never wholly cleared up. But these difficulties with regard to details are discounted as serious objections when we remember—a fundamental consideration in this connexion — the aim of the Evangelists in the Gospels. " The narratives constitute not primarily a history, but a Gospel of the Resurrection," and while " incomplete as a history " they may be " complete as a Gospel " (see Westcott, *Revelation of the Risen Lord*, pp. 4, 6). They were written not to create belief in the resurrection of Jesus in the minds of men to whom the fact was unfamiliar, but to inform more fully those who had already received the general

tradition of the Church, and to show the significance of
the fact, both for Him and for them. " Believing in the
resurrection themselves, and writing for those who
believed in it, they [the writers] aimed at giving such
an account of it as should bring out its permanent
significance for the Church " (Denney, *Jesus and the
Gospel*, p. 153). With this in view each writer selects
the facts which he considers most appropriate to his
object. He is so far indifferent to their connexion with
other facts which he is not concerned to relate. He
may pass over a great part of the evidence, or he may
mass it together in a generalized statement ; and, while
he will not consciously depart from historical truthful-
ness, he will yet so handle his materials that, in order
to estimate them aright, we must keep distinctly before
us his special aim.

The different interests or points of view of the
Evangelists will determine the perspective in which the
facts are viewed, and the different aspects of the facts
emphasized. Matthew, *e.g.*, is occupied throughout his
Gospel with the Galilæan ministry of Jesus as that in
which he beheld the fulfilment of Jewish prophecy.
So in his account of the Appearings he concentrates on
the meeting in Galilee with its great commission, " Go
ye therefore, and make disciples of all the nations."
To this as his objective he hastens on without paus-
ing on intermediate events. While Matthew thus concentrates on the meeting in Galilee, Luke, on the other
hand, is chiefly interested in the Appearings in
Jerusalem on the Resurrection day as leading up to the
promise of the Spirit and the Ascension at Bethany, and

ignores the Appearings in Galilee. "We do the Evangelists injustice," therefore, "when we regard them as witnesses in a court of law, who have been appointed to prove a fact, and who have deliberately taken it in hand to do so" (W. Milligan, *The Resurrection of our Lord*, p. 57). Not that the narratives are not evidence, but they are not put forward as presenting the complete evidence. There is not the least ground for supposing that the Evangelists told us all they knew, nor yet the least necessity that they should have done so. They recorded what was sufficient for their purpose. To bring out the meaning or significance of the Appearings to the disciples, they may have condensed into a single representative or typical scene what they knew to be different Appearings.

Thus we find that even so conservative a critic as Denney counts it "not in the least improbable . . . that in the great appearing of Jesus to the eleven recorded in all the gospels (Matt. xxviii. 16–20; Mark xvi. 14–18; Luke xxiv. 36–49; John xx. 19–23) we have not the literal record of what took place on a single occasion, but the condensation into a representative scene of all that the appearances of Jesus to His disciples meant. . . . And if Jesus nevertheless had in point of fact appeared in different places, we can understand how one evangelist should put this typical scene in Galilee and another in Jerusalem. When we see what is being done we should rather say that both are right than that either is wrong" (*Jesus and the Gospel*, p. 155 f.). The main thing in all the narratives is not the details of time or place or circumstances—in regard to these a certain confusion may remain through unassimilated and un-harmonized traditions—but the fact of the appearing of the Risen Christ to His disciples, together with the significance of the fact. And to establish this, to justify and sustain the faith that Jesus is risen from the dead, the narratives, though fragmentary and in no case presenting an orderly statement of the whole facts, supply sufficient evidence. So that Sanday, while recognizing to the full the difficulties in the narratives, yet maintains that " no difficulty of weaving the separate incidents into an orderly well-compacted narrative can impugn the unanimous belief of the Church which lies behind them, that the Lord Jesus Christ rose from the dead on the third day and appeared to the disciples " (art. " Jesus Christ " in Hastings' *Dict. of Bible*, ii. 641ª).

This enables us also to answer the other objections brought against the apostolic narratives—that the appearances recorded were only to the circle of His disciples, to " interested parties," and, therefore, that the evidence presented is not of a kind to satisfy the demands of scientific historical inquiry. This objection, urged, as we have seen above, by Strauss and Renan, is one which occurs already in Celsus' criticism of Chris-tianity written about the end of the second century. " After these points," says Origen, taking up Celsus' objections one by one, " Celsus proceeds to bring against the Gospel narratives a charge which is not to be lightly passed over, viz. that if Jesus desired to convince men that He was really divine He ought to have appeared to those who had ill-treated Him, and to him who had condemned Him, and to men generally ($\mathring{o}\lambda\omega\varsigma$ $\pi\hat{a}\sigma\iota\nu$) "

(*c. Cels.* ii. 63). The fact to which this criticism refers is, it should be noted, explicitly acknowledged by the apostles. "Him," says Peter, "God raised on the third day, and allowed him to be seen not by all the people but by witnesses whom God had previously selected, by us who ate and drank with him after his resurrection from the dead" (Acts x. 40 f. [Moffatt]). The evidence was designed not to satisfy "scientific experts," but to evoke and support belief in the Resurrection on the part of those "whom God had previously selected" that they might be "witnesses" to others. If the fact to be testified to were the manner of the Resurrection and the exact sequence of the physical changes that accompanied it, supposing this capable of description in scientific terms, then, no doubt, the disciples were not qualified witnesses. They were born 1900 years too soon for this. But "if the essential truth to be conveyed was the personal identity of Him who died and was buried with Him who was raised and appeared, what evidence is to be compared with that of intimate personal friends?" (*Cambridge Theol. Essays*, p. 323). To impugn their witness as not impartial is to forget what the narratives uniformly testify, that, so far from being predisposed to believe in the fact, their predisposition was all the other way.

There are two other considerations which may be brought forward in support of the restriction of the appearings of the Risen Christ to His disciples. (i.) This limitation or restriction is in keeping with Christ's manifestations during His earthly life. To appear to outsiders, to His opponents or enemies or men

generally, in order to convince them of His resurrection
and thus turn them to belief in Him, would have been
contrary to the principle whereby He consistently
refused to present miraculous proofs in order to force
unwilling belief.   When on one occasion the Pharisees
asked Him to give them a sign which should remove
their unbelief, we read that " He sighed deeply in his
spirit, and said, Why doth this generation seek a sign ?
verily I say unto you, There shall no sign be given unto
this generation " (Mark viii. 12).   Faith induced b
such signs was not of the proper quality (cf. Luke
xvi. 31).   This is not the kind of evidence that
convinces.   True faith is morally and spiritually conditioned.   The principle which governed the action of
Jesus on earth in His manifestation of Himself still
determined the action of the Risen Christ.   " Why is
it that you are to appear to us and not to the world ?
. . . If any one loves me . . . we will come to him "
(John xiv. 22 f.).   (ii.) Especially is this the case when
we remember that the purpose of the Appearings was
not merely to convince of identity but to reveal a new
order of life.   If the Resurrection were simply a return
to life under normal conditions, the mere survival of
death, the objection urged might have more weight.
Outsiders, " men generally," can tell whether a man who
is dead at one moment has returned the next to a normal
human life.   But the resurrection of Jesus was a rising
to life under new and more spiritual conditions, the
revelation of a new kind of life, and because of this it
could appeal only to those who were capable of receiving
such truth.   Such a revelation could be received, its

significance could be appreciated, only by those of spiritual receptiveness, who had the faculties to discern the possibilities of a new life in Him. Only they were competent witnesses. Here we are in a realm where the scientific expert is not the expert in the case.

There are those who go the length of maintaining that the resurrection-body of Jesus was in its very nature such as required a spiritual susceptibility to discern, making it impossible for the outward senses alone to recognize its existence. Westcott, *e.g.*, says, "If it [the Resurrection] was a foreshadowing of new powers of human action, of a new mode of human being, then without a corresponding power of spiritual discernment there could be no testimony to its truth. The world could not see Christ, and Christ could not— there is a Divine impossibility—shew Himself to the world" (*Revelation of the Risen Lord*, p. 11 ; cf. *The Gospel of the Resurrection*, p. 162 f., "Human sense alone was not capable of discerning Who He was "). But even if such a manifestation could have been made it would have been valueless for the purpose in view in the manifestations. "Even if the world could have visibly recognised the identity of the risen with the earthly Jesus, yet it could have had no perception of what His risen life meant, seeing that the transformation in Him, which was quite as real and essential as the identity, required spiritual receptivity for the discernment of its significance " (Forrest, *The Christ of History and of Experience*[7], p. 156 n.).

LITERATURE.—B. F. Westcott, *Gospel of the Resurrection*[6], London, 1888, ch. i., *Revelation of the Risen Lord*[2], do., 1882 ; W. Milligan,

Resurrection of our Lord, do., 1881, lect. ii. ; **W. Sanday,** *Outlines of the Life of Christ*[2], Edinburgh, 1906, art. "Jesus Christ," Hastings' *Dict. of Bible,* ii. 638–642 ; **R. J. Knowling,** *Witness of the Epistles,* London, 1892, *Testimony of St. Paul to Christ,* do., 1905 ; **A. C. McGiffert,** *A History of Christianity in the Apostolic Age,* Edinburgh, 1897, pp. 39–44, 55 f. ; **F. Loofs,** *Die Auferstehungsberichte und ihr Wert,* Leipzig, 1898 ; **E. von Dobschütz,** *Ostern und Pfingsten,* do., 1903 ; **P. W. Schmiedel,** "Resurrection- and Ascension-Narratives" in *Encycl. Bibl.* iv. 4039–4087 ; "The Evidence for the Resurrection of Christ" in *Church Quarterly Review,* lxi. [1906] 323 ff. ; **K. Lake,** *The Historical Evidence for the Resurrection of Jesus Christ,* London, 1907 ; **H. B. Swete,** *The Appearances of our Lord after the Passion,* do., 1907 ; **J. Denney,** *Jesus and the Gospel,* do., 1908, pp. 107–159 ; **J. M. Thompson,** *Miracles in the New Testament,* do., 1911, pp. 161–205 ; **F. H. Chase,** *The Gospels in the Light of Historical Criticism,* do., 1914, p. 39 ff. ; **T. J. Thorburn,** *The Resurrection Narratives and Modern Criticism,* do., 1910 (a criticism of Schmiedel's art. in *Encycl. Bibl.*) ; **W. P. Armstrong,** "The Place of the Resurrection Appearances of Jesus" in *Biblical and Theological Studies* (Princeton), New York, 1912, p. 307 ff. ; **W. J. Sparrow Simpson,** *Our Lord's Resurrection,* London, 1905, chs. i.–vii., *The Resurrection and Modern Thought,* do., 1911, bks. i. and ii. ; **R. H. Hutton,** *Theological Essays*[4], do., 1895, Essay vi. "Christian Evidences, Popular and Critical," and Essay viii. "The Incarnation and Principles of Evidence."

CHAPTER V

THE APOSTOLIC WITNESS TO THE NATURE
OF CHRIST'S RESURRECTION-BODY

THAT the grave was found empty on the third day,
that on the same day He appeared to His disciples,
and that these appearings, succeeding upon the empty
grave, had already given rise on the third day to a
belief in the Resurrection, are facts historically well
attested by the Gospel narratives and corroborated by
St. Paul's account. But there is more than this. The
appearings of the Risen Christ were, according to the
apostolic witness, not mere appearings and nothing
more; they were in the nature of interviews or conver-
sations, sometimes for a considerable length of time,
between Him and His disciples. "There is no such
thing in the New Testament as an appearance of the
Risen Saviour in which He merely appears. He is
always represented as entering into relation to those who
see Him in other ways than by a flash upon the inner
or the outer eye: He establishes other communications
between Himself and His own than that which can
be characterised in this way" (Denney, *Death of Christ*,
London, 1902, p. 67). And the apostolic narratives
bear witness to a certain view of the nature or mode of
existence of the Risen Christ.

I. THE WITNESS OF THE GOSPELS

In the picture given in the Gospel narratives we have a noteworthy combination of seemingly opposite qualities in the Risen Christ's mode of existence.

(*a*) On the one hand, Christ seemed to have resumed the form of bodily existence maintained while on earth. His mode of existence was not phantasmal or apparitional like a ghost, but embodied. He appeared in a body possessing attributes and functions which attested its physical reality and identity (or continuity) with the former earthly body.

(1) He could be seen, touched, handled, as a purely spiritual existence could not (Luke xxiv. 39 f.; John xx. 20). Indeed we are told that He offered Himself to their touch and handling to convince the disciples of His bodily existence: "Feel me and see; a ghost has not flesh and bones as you see I have" (Luke xxiv. 39 [Moffatt]; cf. John xx. 20). Or, as another report has it, coming either from the *Gospel according to the Hebrews* or from the *Doctrine of Peter*: "Take handle me and see that I am not a bodiless spirit" (Ignatius, *Smyrn.* 3, λάβετε, ψηφαλήσατέ με, καὶ ἴδετε ὅτι οὐκ εἰμὶ δαιμόνιον ἀσώματον). On "flesh and bones" Westcott says: "The significant variation from the common formula 'flesh and blood' must have been at once intelligible to Jews, accustomed to the provisions of the Mosaic ritual, and nothing would have impressed upon them more forcibly the transfiguration of Christ's Body than the verbal omission of the element of blood which was for them the symbol and seat of corruptible

life" (*Gospel of the Resurrection,* p. 162 n.).   We are not told that the disciples availed themselves of the test at Jesus' invitation.   But in Matt. xxviii. 9 we read, "They [the women] took hold of his feet and worshipped him."   If the disciples did not actually touch Him it was, it would seem, because "they were so convinced, by sight, of His reality, that they abstained out of reverence from subjecting Him to the further test" (Forrest, *The Christ of Hist. and of Exper.*[7], p. 148 n.).

The body was apparently capable also of partaking of food, for we are told that as they were still incredulous and "wondered," He took a piece of a broiled fish which remained from the evening meal and ate before them (Luke xxiv. 41–43; the words "and of a honeycomb" are omitted by the best MSS.).   This touch in the incident, which is mentioned only by Luke, has been called in question by Loofs and others as "secondary" and "representing the more realistic shape which the legend of the Resurrection ultimately took."   Even Denney shares this doubt: "There does seem something which is not only incongruous but repellent in the idea of the Risen Lord eating," and he finds in it one illustration of Luke's "tendency to materialise the spiritual" (*Jesus and the Gospel,* p. 146).   In support of this it has been noted that in the case of the meal with the two disciples at Emmaus (Luke xxiv. 30), and in the later scene of the seven beside the Lake recorded in John xxi. 4–13, it is not said in either case that Jesus Himself partook of the bread which He distributed to others with His own hand.   If we retain this touch, we must say with Clement of Alexandria, "He did not eat

6

for the sake of His body, but for their sakes with whom
He conversed," to convince them that they were not
seeing a ghost. "If there be resurrection of the body,
there is no reason why such a body should not have the
power of taking food without depending on it" (E. R.
Bernard, Hastings' *Dict. of Bible*, iv. 234ᵃ). But even
if we eliminate this detail in the picture, which ad-
mittedly is the least certain element in it, the picture
in its essentials is not appreciably altered. The Risen
Christ's mode of existence was such that human eyes
could see and human hands could touch and feel Him.

(2) Further, the body in which He appeared was a
body identical (or continuous) with the body which He
had on earth, and which had suffered on the Cross and
been laid in the tomb. Apart from the fact that the
grave in which the body of Jesus had been laid on the
Friday evening was found empty on the morning of
the third day, identity (or continuity) was evidenced
by the fact that the Risen Body bore the marks of
the Passion, the print of the nails in the hands, and
the spear-mark in the side (Luke xxiv. 39 f.; John
xx. 27).

Luke xxiv. 40, καὶ τοῦτο εἰπὼν ἔδειξεν αὐτοῖς τὰς χεῖρας καὶ τοὺς
πόδας, is called in question as omitted in some authorities, but John
xx. 20, where probably the same appearance is described though
there is a seeming discrepancy in the number of disciples present,
is undoubted. See Plummer, *Internat. Crit. Comm.*, "St. Luke"²,
Edinburgh, 1898, *in loc.*

The identity, it would seem, extended still further.
Mary recognized Him by the familiar tone of the voice
(John xx. 16) and the two disciples by the familiar
gesture in the breaking of bread (Luke xxiv. 31).

(*b*) On the other hand, the body if the same was yet somehow not the same. It had undergone some marvellous change. If there was identity, there was yet contrast. The Risen Body had mysterious peculiarities which distinguished it from the natural earthly body. Indeed, so prominent were these distinguishing peculiarities that the Risen Lord is uniformly represented in the narrative as with difficulty persuading the disciples of the identity of the two. Chief of these peculiarities are—

(1) *The transcendence of the ordinary laws of material or physical existence.*—Matter was no longer an obstacle. The Risen Christ could pass through a closed sepulchre (apparently implied by Matt. xxviii. 2) and through shut doors (Luke xxiv. 36 ; John xx. 19–26). Distance could not delay His movements; He could be present in different and distant places at short intervals (Luke xxiv. 15, 34). Suddenly He appears without apparent physical locomotion (Luke xxiv. 36 ; John xx. 19, 26, "Jesus stood [ἔστη] in the midst"). As suddenly He disappears (Luke xxiv. 31, "He vanished from their sight," ἄφαντος ἐγένετο ἀπ᾽ αὐτῶν—a disappearance, not a spatial withdrawal). Here apparently is an emerging from and a withdrawal into complete invisibility at will. It was not distance that made Him seen or unseen. He did not go away ; He only disappeared. He really did not come ; He but made Himself manifest. And then, finally, as illustrating this transcendence of the ordinary laws of material existence, we are told He ascended from earth to heaven in visible form (Luke xxiv. 51 ; Acts i. 9 ; cf. Mark xvi. 19).

The words καὶ ἀνεφέρετο εἰς τὸν οὐρανόν in Luke xxiv. 51 and all ver. 19 in Mark xvi. are regarded as doubtful by textual criticism, and, even if they be accepted, it has been contended that they do not of themselves imply a visible ascent (see E. P. Gould in *Internat. Crit. Comm.*, "St. Mark," Edinburgh, 1896, p. 309). But such a visible ascent is directly stated in Luke's second treatise, Acts i. 9 f., and the subsequent joy of the disciples (Luke xxiv. 52 f.) distinctly points to some such visible representation of His final triumph over death (cf. Forrest, *The Christ of Hist. and of Exper.*[7], p. 413).

(2) *Difficulty of recognition from mere outward appearances.*—So great was the change that, it would seem, the mere external form and features failed to disclose who He was, even to those with whom He had had familiar intercourse on earth. Mary Magdalene mistook Him for the gardener, until He called her by her name (John xx. 14–16). The two men on the way to Emmaus not only walked but conversed with Him for a considerable length of time, yet did not know who He was till He was made known to them in the breaking of bread (Luke xxiv. 30–32). When He stood in the midst of the assembled disciples He seemed so strange to them that they "imagined it was a ghost they saw" and they were "scared and terrified" till "he showed them his hands and feet" (Luke xxiv. 37–40 [Moffatt]; cf. John xx. 20, "his hands and his side"). And again, at the Sea of Tiberias, when Jesus stood on the beach, the disciples (among whom were four apostles) failed to recognize Him (John xxi. 4).

This is the more striking when we consider (i.) that the appearances were not momentary glimpses, but, at least in several of the cases, prolonged interviews; and (ii.) that even when He appeared to the same people a

second or third time they were still at first perplexed
and had their doubts as to His identity.   What was the
cause of this non-recognition ?   It may be that the
failure of Mary Magdalene to recognize Jesus at the
beginning was due, as some maintain, to her eyes being
dimmed with tears, and her mind bewildered and
perplexed—this, combined with the dimness of the
early morning light.   It may be that the two disciples
on the way to Emmaus failed to recognize Him because
of mental preoccupation with their grief, and absorption
in their puzzled discussion of the story told by the
women.   " Their eyes were holden (ἐκρατοῦντο, over-
powered, spellbound) that they should not know him
(τοῦ μὴ ἐπιγνῶναι αὐτόν)," says Luke in explanation
(xxiv. 16).   These words need not be taken to imply
any special supernatural action on their senses on the
part of the Risen Christ, " ' who would not be seen by
them till the time when He saw fit ' " (see Plummer,
Internat. Crit. Comm., in loc.).   They may mean simply
that they did not know Him ; that, through some
conditions on their side, they failed to recognize Him
(cf. Moffatt's translation, " they were prevented from
recognizing him ").   It has to be remembered that in this
case neither of the two, so far as we know, belonged to
the company of the apostles, and if they never before
had come into close quarters with the Master, their
failure to recognize Him, it is held, was not surprising
(cf. Swete, *Appearances*, p. 23).   Once more, in the
incident at the Lake of Tiberias the words of the
Evangelist, " when early morn was now arrived, *or*
arriving " (πρωίας δὲ ἤδη γενομένης, other MSS. γινομένης),

suggest that the disciples may have been hindered from recognizing Jesus on the shore by the dimness of the dawning morning light.   These and such-like conditions may have contributed to the effect.   Their mental condition in particular has to be taken into account as an operating factor in the case.   It is altogether probable that their surprise and bewilderment, combined with their hopeless grief, made them less capable of exact observation than in ordinary circumstances.   Yet the narratives convey the impression that there was something more in the case than this; that some mysterious change had occurred in Jesus' outward appearance which at least assisted non-recognition and excited awe in the beholders (Luke xxiv. 37); that some change in bodily appearance had taken place corresponding to the mysterious change already referred to in Christ's relation to ordinary physical laws.

"He appeared to them in another form" (ἐν ἑτέρᾳ μορφῇ), says the Mark Appendix of the manifestation to the two on the way to Emmaus.   That the words mean only that to the two on the way to Emmaus He presented a different appearance from that to Mary Magdalene (possibly, as Alford suggests, through his dress being changed, giving the impression not now of a gardener or labourer at work, but rather of a traveller with his loins girt, shoes on feet, and staff in hand) is altogether improbable.   The natural interpretation of the words is that He appeared in a different form from that He had on earth, that some change had come over Him so that He did not look the same as when He was with them before the Passion (" μορφή always signifies a form which truly and fully expresses the being which underlies it" [H. A. A. Kennedy, in *Expos. Gk. Test.*, London, 1903, on Phil. ii. 6]).

This is supported by the cumulative evidence of the narratives, the uniform testimony of which is that, while the same, some mysterious change had come over His whole mode of existence. It is a change which attaches to all that we read in the Gospels of the appearances of Jesus. It was not only, as we have seen, that His risen body was no longer subject to ordinary physical laws, but the manner of His intercourse with His disciples after His resurrection was altogether changed. His appearances were occasional. He appeared only when He willed to appear. There is a strange aloofness and reserve about His attitude to them. He is no longer their companion as He used to be; He speaks of the time "when I was yet with you" (Luke xxiv. 44). Though He invites them to feel Him that they may be thus convinced that He was no phantasm or apparition, but indeed the Risen Jesus, He forbids Mary Magdalene to "keep clinging to him" (John xx. 17, μή μου ἅπτου) so as to hold Him in possession. The prohibition of Jesus meant that the old earthly intercourse and relations with His disciples which Mary wished to resume could not be restored, that they were for ever past, and that their place was to be taken by a new and higher kind of fellowship, to be realized only when He had completed His earthly self-manifestation, and had "ascended unto the Father" (John xx. 17, οὔπω γὰρ ἀναβέβηκα). For the present He is, in His intercourse with them, hovering between the old and the new in a transitional condition, combining the seemingly opposite qualities of the material and spiritual, embodied " in another form."

This combination of two opposite or at least contrasted sets of characteristics in the appearances of the Risen Christ Weizsäcker (*Apost. Age*[2], i. 9–11) makes the basis of criticism of the credibility of the Gospel accounts. They represent, he says, two different layers of tradition. The appearances were in their earliest form purely spiritual or visional; but, as time went on, the craving for external and palpable signs, combined with popular realistic ideas of a carnal Resurrection, led to a gradual materializing of the visions, and an endowing of the visional with physical attributes, thus overlaying history with legend. So Harnack and others hold that the idea of a bodily Resurrection was a form subsequently imposed on a more primary spiritual belief in the Lord's continued life. Such an overlaying of the Gospel representations by popular realistic conceptions was a process which history shows speedily manifested itself in the early Church. We have it already in the extra-canonical Gospels referred to above, the *Gospel according to the Hebrews* and the *Gospel of Peter*, more explicitly in the Apostolic Fathers and still more definitely in the Apologists— dominating indeed post-Apostolic thought up to the time of Origen. But the combination of contrasted traits—the " dual quality " or double aspect of His appearances—is of the very essence of the Gospel accounts throughout, present in what Weizsäcker terms the earlier layers of the tradition as really as in the later. And if the Resurrection be what it is uniformly represented in the narratives as being—not the simple reanimation of His mortal body which Harnack speaks of (*Hist. of Dogma*, i. 85 n.), a resuscitation and restoration to the former conditions of existence, but the entrance on a new order of life,—then the combination in the Gospel accounts of the Appearings of apparently inconsistent aspects, so far from casting doubt on these accounts, is a strong evidence of their historical trustworthiness.

For such a conception of the mode of existence of the Risen Christ the disciples had absolutely no precedent. On the contrary, it was to them, as the records show, a most novel and strange idea for which they were unprepared, and which with difficulty they were persuaded to receive. It was opposed to both Jewish and Greek ideas on the subject. The Resurrection as it actually took place " would be quite foreign to Jewish ideas, which embraced the continuance of the soul after death and the final resurrection of the body, but not a state of spiritual corporeity, far less, under conditions such as those described in the Gospels " (Edersheim, *Life and Times of Jesus the Messiah*[4], ii. 624). About the current Palestinian Jewish conception of the Resurrection-Body there was little that was spiritual. " The future body, as to material and organisation, was conceived as essentially of the same quality as the present " (F. W. Weber, *Lehren des Talmud*, Leipzig, 1880, p. 353, quoted by Kennedy, *St. Paul's Conceptions of the Last Things*, p. 227). In *Apoc. Bar.* (*e.g.* l. 2) it is stated that the bodies of the dead shall be raised exactly as they were when committed to the ground. After this has been done for purposes of recognition by friends, a glorious change will indeed take place: "they shall be made like unto the angels, and be made equal to the stars, and they shall be changed into every form they desire from beauty into loveliness, and from light into the splendour of glory" (li. 10 ; cf. the more spiritual ideas prominent in *Enoch, e.g.* l. 4, civ. 4, 6, cviii. 11, etc.). The changed body is still, however, described largely in sensuous physical terms, while here, in the case of the Risen Christ, was a body so spiritualized that they thought it was a spirit. On the other hand, the Alexandrian Greek conception was that of emancipation from the body and continued existence as pure spirit. But, besides the fact that the tomb was empty, here was a body which could be not only seen but touched and felt, and presented evident marks of identity with the body of earth. "Feel me and see, a spirit hath not flesh and bones as you see me have" (Luke xxiv. 39). The marvel of the records is the perfect simplicity, the perfect naturalness with which the two sets of characteristics are combined in the same narratives, "as if those who put the facts together were conscious of no difficulty in the apparent contradiction" (Westcott, *Gospel of the Resurrection*, p. ix). If we take one series of events, the Resurrection might appear to have been a mere coming back to life; if we take another, it might appear to be purely spiritual or spiritualistic. But the records combine both, and thus differentiate the apostolic representation of the resurrection of Jesus from the two current conceptions—from the sensuous conception of it held by the Pharisees, and from the spiritualistic conception of the Alexandrian or Greek philosophers.

Such a representation had no precedent, and can be explained only by the new revelation conveyed to the disciples through the appearings and intercourse of the Risen Christ, as recorded for us in the narratives. Through these Appearings or self-manifestations Christ sought to impress on His disciples, on the one hand, the identity of the Risen with the Crucified Jesus, and on the other, that His resurrection was not a mere restoration to life but a triumph of His whole personality, body and spirit, over death and His entrance on a new and higher mode of existence. So Jesus offered Himself to the senses of the disciples, even to their touch and handling, if this were needed to convince them of His identity—even, it may be, to the eating of bread, if thereby the feeling that He was a phantasm or apparition could be more completely removed. These manifestations of our Lord's risen body to the senses of His disciples were evidential in character and purpose, an accommodation to the disciples' incredulity, temporarily granted in order the better to establish the fact of His identity. (Cf. Chrysostom, Hom. lxxxvii. in *Ev. Ioan.*, Library of the Fathers, p. 782: "What took place was a matter of condescension . . . that the Resurrection might be believed, and that man might know that it was the Crucified One Himself, and that another rose not in His stead"). But when this was attained, when doubt of His identity was removed and the disciples thought to resume the old familiar intercourse, He manifested the characteristics of a more spiritual form of existence, and they learned the truth that the Resurrection was the entrance on a new order of life and

a higher kind of fellowship.   So the Ascension is represented in the Gospel narratives as the natural and
necessary sequel of the Resurrection.   The visible lifting
from the earth marked the close of the visible intercourse
and the beginning of the more spiritual for which the disciples were gradually prepared by the teaching of the forty
days (John xx. 17 ; cf. Luke xxiv. 49 ; Acts i. 8 ;
John xiv.–xvi.) (see Denney, art. " Ascension," Hastings'
Dict. of Bible, i. 161 ; cf. Westcott, *Revelation of the Risen
Lord*, p. 160 : " The change which Christ revealed by the
Ascension was not a change of place but a change of
state, not local but spiritual " ; and *Gospel of the Resurrection*, p. 288 : " The Ascension finally interprets the
Resurrection for men, and under the forms of common
thought.   The visible lifting from the earth marked the
close of one epoch of revelation and the beginning of
another "). The contention (*e.g.* Newman Smyth, *Old
Faiths in New Light*, London, n.d., p. 156 f.) that the
body of Jesus during the forty days underwent a gradual
process of spiritualization or glorification, a " process of
resurrection," which was consummated in the Ascension
does not seem to be supported by the narratives.   On the
very day of His resurrection the spirituality of His
risen body was as manifest as in the case of the appearance by the Sea of Tiberias (cf. Luke xxiv. 31, 36 ;
John xxi. 4 ff. ; see Forrest, *Christ of Hist. and of Exper.*[7],
p. 411 f.).

With the question of the essential or intrinsic nature
of the Resurrection-Body the Evangelists were not
concerned, so much as with that of the nature of the
appearances or self-manifestations of this Body during

the forty days.   They are describing actual historical manifestations, not going behind these manifestations to analyze the nature of the Resurrection-Body as it is in itself.   This latter is St. Paul's contribution to the witness.   For this reason, and because of the evidential purpose of the appearances of the Risen Body during the forty days, we cannot argue simply from them to the essential normal characteristics of the Risen Body. But from the temporary manifestations of the Risen Body during the forty days there were two things, either of which they might have thought it to be, which they came to know it was not.   It was not simply the old earthly body resumed, and it was not a mere phantasmal existence.   And one thing they knew it was—it was a body no longer subject to physical limitations and restrictions, but completely under the control of the spiritual nature or will; so completely under control that it could manifest itself in such material form or forms as were necessary for evidential purposes. Already during the earthly ministry there were, according to the Gospels, pre-glimpses of this control of body by spirit.   Two of the best attested incidents in the narratives—His walking on the water and the Trans-figuration—are instances in point (cf. Swete, *Appearances*, p. 24).   The chief significance of the Transfiguration has been found by some to consist just in this, that it was meant to prepare the disciples for the Resurrection and for the appearance of the Risen Jesus in glorified form (see, *e.g.*, H. A. A. Kennedy in *Journal of Theol. Stud.* iv. [1903] 270 ff.).   The removal of the stone from the door of the tomb, recorded in Matt. xxviii. 2, which is sometimes used to support a physical view of the Resurrection as consisting in a reanimation and resuscitation of the natural body, if necessary was so only for evidential purposes—not to let Christ out but to let the disciples in and convince them that the tomb was empty.

CHAPTER VI

THE APOSTOLIC WITNESS TO THE NATURE OF CHRIST'S RESURRECTION-BODY (*Continued*)

II. THE WITNESS OF ST. PAUL

ST. PAUL'S view of the resurrection-body of Christ is derived for the most part indirectly, chiefly by way of inference from and implication in his teaching as to the nature of the resurrection-body of Christians as given especially in 1 Cor. xv. His description of this body as "spiritual" is but the further elucidation and interpretation of the teaching of the forty days, and is intelligible only against the background of the empty tomb and the manifestations of Christ's risen body, reports of which he would receive from first-hand witnesses — that supplemented by and interpreted through Christ's appearance to himself in His risen form on the Damascus road.

In regard to the Risen Body St. Paul holds firmly the two points borne witness to by the Gospel accounts :

(1) The identity between the body which was buried and the body which was raised. Some critics maintain that there is no identity between the two in St. Paul's teaching, and that St. Paul was indifferent to the question of the empty grave (cf. above, p. 15 ff.). But the very

words "that Christ died . . . and that he was buried and that he hath been raised on the third day" (1 Cor. xv. 3 f.) are, as Feine points out (*Theol. des NT*, p. 362), susceptible of no other interpretation than that of identity. The insertion of the clause "and that he was buried" between "died" and "raised on the third day" emphasizes the identity between the Body that was buried and the Body that was raised glorified and spiritualized. Even Schmiedel concedes this: "That Jesus was buried and that 'he has been raised' (1 Cor. xv. 4) cannot be affirmed by any one who has not the reanimation of the body in mind" (*Encycl. Bibl.* iv. 4059). In like manner Lake: "There can be clearly no doubt that he (St. Paul) believed in the complete personal identity of that which rose with that which had died and been buried" (*Resurrection of Jesus Christ*, p. 20). This belief is unambiguously implied also in the Apostle's statements in other Epistles, *e.g.* Rom. viii. 11: "If the spirit of him that raised up Jesus from the dead dwelleth in you, he that raised up Christ Jesus from the dead shall quicken also your mortal bodies through his spirit that dwelleth in you," where the "mortal body" is plainly referred to as the subject of the quickening (cf. 1 Cor. vi. 14).

(2) Equally with identity, however, the difference between the two Bodies is insisted on, represented analogically by the distinction (made in arguing for the resurrection of believers) between the seed and the perfected plant: "Thou sowest not that body that shall be" (ver. 37). [The analogy of the seed is employed, it should be noted, to illustrate and emphasize not so

much the identity as the difference between the body
sown and raised.]   St. Paul speaks of the risen body of
believers as a body not of flesh and blood ("flesh and blood
cannot inherit the Kingdom of God," ver. 50), but one
transfigured and transformed, "made like unto the body
of Christ's glory" (Phil. iii. 21), the body of the Risen
and Exalted Lord.   A distinction is drawn between the
"psychical" or "natural" body (σῶμα ψυχικόν) and the
"pneumatical" or "spiritual" body (σῶμα πνευματικόν),
the former the vehicle of self-manifestation under earthly
conditions, the latter the organ of self-manifestation
under supra-terrestrial conditions.   The difference consists not in the body being changed into spirit but in
its being entirely subjected to the dominion or control of
the spirit.   Thus the risen body of Christ is described as
spiritual "because in it matter was wholly and finally sub-
jugated to spirit, and not to the exigencies of physical
life.   Matter no longer restricted Him or hindered.
It had become the pure and transparent vehicle of
spiritual purpose" (Gore, *Body of Christ*, p. 127).   (For
fuller statement of St. Paul's view and for the striking
corroboration of St. Paul's conception of the "spiritual
body" supplied by recent science, see below, p. 144 ff.)

In one important respect indeed a difference is recog-
nized by St. Paul between the resurrection-body of
Christ and that of believers. The natural body of
Christ unlike that of His followers saw no corruption.
In their speeches in Acts both St. Peter and St. Paul
call special attention to the uniqueness of Christ's
experience in this particular respect—that He the Holy
One was not suffered to see corruption (Acts ii. 31,

7

xiii. 34 f.).   The body of earth, the body which was crucified and buried, was not left in the tomb to undergo dissolution, but was raised transfigured and transformed into a spiritual incorruptible body " in such a way," as Lake acknowledges, " that there was no trace left of the corruptible body of flesh and blood which had been laid in the grave " (*Resurrection of Jesus Christ*, p. 20).   This in Christ's case was necessary, to begin with, for evidential ends—necessary, *i.e.*, if men were to believe in the reality of His resurrection and the completeness of His triumph over death and the grave. If Christ's natural body had remained in the tomb, no demonstration had been given sufficient to convince the disciples of His complete victory over death and His entrance through it on a new and higher mode of existence.   But not only was it thus necessary for evidential purposes that Christ's body should not be allowed to remain in the grave to see corruption; it was, it would seem, according to the Apostolic view and, as we shall argue later (see p. 203 ff.), according to the very reason of things altogether natural and in the very nature of the case that a body unstained by sin such as that of Jesus was should not be abandoned in death.   In our case the " redemption of the body " (Rom. viii. 23) involves the laying aside of the tainted body of earth, leaving it in the grave to the process of dissolution and decay, in order to our being clothed with a body which shall be a fit habitation for the spirit—a body whose identity with that of earth is the identity not of material elements but of the same individual vital principle organizing both (cf. Westcott, *Gospel of the Resurrection*,

p. 144 f.). In the case of Christ, however, no such abandonment was needed, inasmuch as the body of earth was already the complete servant of spirit. The body of flesh was indeed not simply revivified and resuscitated, after the manner of the other raisings from the dead recorded in the Bible—that was the form of belief in the Resurrection which became practically universal in post-Apostolic and mediæval times, finding expression in the phrase "the resurrection of the flesh"—rather it was quickened and raised up to a new order of existence, transfigured and transformed without being abandoned. Cf. Bernard in *Expositor*, 7th ser., v. 500 (1908): "After death His σῶμα ψυχικόν was quickened into the σῶμα πνευματικόν, the body of His glory, the action of the Divine Spirit being so overmasteringly efficacious that no sensuous or fleshly element was left behind in the sepulchre. It was transfigured and transformed, the body of earth being in His case, even throughout His earthly progress, a fit habitation for the πνεῦμα. For sin had never defiled it nor had temptation ever thwarted the activities of the spirit of Christ." In respect of this important difference, it is not strictly true to say, as Milligan does (*Resurrection of our Lord*, p. 18), that "our Lord's resurrection is the type and model of our own."

As to how the natural body of Jesus became transformed under the Spirit's working, how the spiritual body sprang from the natural under the influence of the Spirit, St. Paul does not attempt to explain further than saying, "It is the power of God" (see below, p. 146). Latham says, "the body exhaled or evanesced" (*Risen Master*, p. 36). If asked, however, "How do you explain this vanishing from the tomb of the material flesh and bones of Christ and change into something which has all the phenomena without the substance of a human body?" his answer, he says, is,

"I do not explain it at all" (*ib.* p. 18). And indeed here we come quickly upon mystery, upon that which transcends our present experience and ability to explain or understand. But as Armitage Robinson reminds us, such mystery is "not peculiar to Religion : it accompanies all investigations of life even upon its lowest levels" (*Journal of Theol. Stud.* xiv. 203).

St. Paul's view has been contrasted with that of the Evangelists as less materialistic, and the difference has been traced to the more spiritual character of the appearance of the Risen Christ to St. Paul as compared with those to the older apostles. But we have to remember the difference of relationship to the Risen Lord between St. Paul and the older disciples. That St. Paul had ever seen Jesus during His earthly life and ministry is doubtful. Ramsay, C. Clemen (*Paulus*, Giessen, 1904), and J. Weiss (*Paulus und Jesus*, Berlin, 1909), among recent critics, maintain that he had. The weight of probability, however, is against the supposition (see Feine, *Jesus Christus und Paulus*, Leipzig, 1902, pp. 93, 350). (2 Cor. v. 16 cannot be cited for or against, for what St. Paul is contrasting here is the knowledge of Christ " after the flesh " [not " in the flesh "] with the knowledge of Him after the spirit— the difference between the estimate of Christ formed by St. Paul before his conversion and after.) Recognition of identity under changed conditions was not, therefore, the primary requirement in St. Paul's case, as it was in the case of the older apostles. The aim of the Appearing to him was to convince him that the Jesus who was crucified and whose followers he persecuted was indeed the Risen and Exalted Christ. To him, therefore, Christ was manifested in the majesty of His Divine glory, a Figure invested in dazzling splendour, with none of those more tangible characteristics which He manifested to the earlier apostles and which seemed necessary for evidential purposes. Because of this difference in position and relationship between him and the older apostles, St. Paul in his statement is concerned more with the normal intrinsic nature of the Resurrection-Body, and less with the temporary self-manifestations of this Body under sensible conditions for evidential ends with which, as we have seen, the Evangelists were primarily concerned. The overlooking of this fact is responsible largely for assertions as to "inconsistency" or "contradiction" between St. Paul and the Evangelists (cf. Sparrow Simpson, *Our Lord's Resurrection*, p. 167 f.).

The question has been raised whether St. Paul derived his view of the Resurrection-Body entirely from what he had seen and heard of the Risen Lord, or was partly influenced by contemporary Jewish or Hellenistic ideas. Lake, *e.g.* (*Resurrection of Jesus Christ*, p. 23 ff.), maintains that "the Pauline doctrine of a transubstantiation of the body at the resurrection is one which was in the main familiar to the Jews," yet he recognizes the influence on St. Paul's doctrine of "his knowledge of appearances of the Risen Lord in the light of which knowledge he re-formed his ideas on the resurrection generally." The question of the influence on St. Paul's doctrine of Christ's own teaching on the resurrection has also to be considered. Feine (*Jesus Christus und Paulus*, p. 181 f.) points out certain remarkable similarities between St. Paul's teaching in 1 Cor. and the narratives of our Lord's discussion with the Sadducees in Mark xii. 18 f.;

Luke xx. 27 f.   The condition of the risen is described by Jesus as being "as the angels of God in heaven" (Mark xii. 25, ὡς ἄγγελοι ἐν τοῖς οὐρανοῖς), or, "like the angels" (ἰσάγγελοι), and as being "sons of God, being sons of the resurrection" (Luke xx. 36).   That is to say, they possess a heavenly or spiritual organism, and are conformed to the likeness of God (see Kennedy, *St. Paul's Conceptions of the Last Things*, pp. 100, 234). This Christian tradition of Jesus' eschatological teaching, if received by St. Paul, was, however, illumined and defined by the manifestations of Jesus to himself and to the other apostles.   Others maintain (*e.g.* Reitzenstein ; see J. Weiss, on 1 Cor. xv. 44) that St. Paul's contrast between the "natural body" (σῶμα ψυχικόν) and the "spiritual body" (σῶμα πνευματικόν) was derived from the Greek mystery-religions.   But the Greek antithesis is based on a dualistic conception of human nature, and St. Paul's contrast is in quite a different category.

LITERATURE.—On the Resurrection-Body see **E. M. Goulburn,** *The Resurrection of the Body as taught in Holy Scripture* (*Bampton Lects.*), London, 1850 ; **B. F. Westcott,** *The Gospel of the Resurrection,* do., 1867, chs. i., ii., *The Revelation of the Risen Lord,* do., 1881, p. 7 ff.; **W. Milligan,** *The Resurrection of our Lord,* do., 1881, Lects. i., ii.; **S. D. F. Salmond's** *Christian Doctrine of Immortality,* Edinburgh, 1895, pp. 568–572 ; **H. Latham,** *The Risen Master,* London, 1900, chs. i.–iii.; **J. H. Skrine,** *Contemporary Review,* lxxxvi. [1904] 860–871 ; "The Resurrection-Body : a Study in the History of Doctrine," *Church Quarterly Review,* lxviii. [1909] 138 ff. ; **R. H. Charles,** *Eschatology, Hebrew, Jewish and Christian,* London, 1899 ; **F. C. Burkitt,** *Jewish and Christian Apocalypses,* do., 1914 ; **R. C. Moberly,** *Problems and Principles,* do. 1904 ; **C. Gore,** *The Body of Christ,* do., 1901 ; **C. H. Robinson,** *Studies in the Resurrection of Christ,* do., 1909, ch. ii. ; **W. J. Sparrow Simpson,** *Our Lord's Resurrection,* do. 1905, ch. viii., *The Resurrection and Modern Thought,* do. 1911, chs. xxiv.–xxix.   Origen's restatement of the Pauline doctrine in *Contra Celsum* (v, 18, 19, 23 *et passim*) should not be overlooked.

CHAPTER VII

THE SIGNIFICANCE OF THE RESURRECTION OF CHRIST FOR APOSTOLIC CHRISTIANITY

THE significance of the Resurrection for the Apostolic Church may be represented under a twofold aspect, (i.) as evidential, (ii.) as essential or constitutive.

I. EVIDENTIAL SIGNIFICANCE

In the older mode of treatment of the Resurrection, in English theology especially, main stress was laid upon its evidential value as the confirmation or proof of the truth of Christ's claims as to His person and work. To place the chief emphasis on this aspect of its significance is to give the Resurrection too abstract and external a character, and is the correlative of that view of the miracles of Jesus natural to eighteenth century theology, which lays stress on their value as credential appendages rather than as an essential part of Jesus' redemptive revelation. According to the invariable apostolic representation, however, the resurrection of Christ is not merely something consequent upon the redemptive revelation of His life and work on earth, something added on to it as the reward and guarantee of its efficacy; it is itself an essential and constitutive part of the revelation, necessary to its culmination or completion. While this is so, the importance of the evidential aspect of the Resurrection is not to be minimized. This is, indeed, where we must begin in our study of the apostolic representation. For the apostles the first and primary significance of the Resurrection lay undoubtedly in the fact that it was the Divine confirmation of Jesus' entire claim as to His person and work. Thus it is—and the importance of the fact has to be noted, as it is often overlooked—that it is always God to whom the apostles impute the raising of Christ. His resurrection was the immediate act of God the Father, Who by this gave His verdict concerning Jesus, thus once for all reversing Israel's act of rejection, and refuting the Jews' charge of blasphemy. "Whom they slew, hanging him on a tree, him God raised up" (Acts x. 39 f.). This is the uniform apostolic representation common to St. Paul and the earlier apostles (cf. Acts ii. 24, 32, 36, iii. 15, iv. 10, v. 31, xiii. 30–39, xvii. 31 ; 1 Thess. i. 10 ; Rom. i. 4, vi. 4 ; 1 Cor. xv. 15 ; Gal. i. 1 ; Eph. i. 20 ; Phil. ii. 9 ; 1 Pet. i. 21 ; Heb. xiii. 20). So that St. Paul says, "If Christ did not rise . . . we are detected bearing false witness to God ($\kappa\alpha\tau\grave{\alpha}$ $\tau o\hat{v}$ $\theta\epsilon o\hat{v}$) by affirming of him that he raised Christ" (1 Cor. xv. 14, 15 [Moffatt]). And if this affirmation or witness is false, then their whole view of the worth of Christ's person and work is without validity. Their preaching of Christ is "empty" (ver. 14) and faith in Him is "vain" (ver. 17). To develop this evidential significance of the Resurrection into its details :

1. *Evidential with regard to His Person*

(*a*) Through the Resurrection conclusive proof was afforded of the *Messiahship* of Jesus. This aspect of its significance was that which was primarily emphasized in the earliest apostolic teaching as represented by the sermons of St. Peter recorded in the early chapters of Acts. That Jesus claimed to be the Messiah, the Divinely sent One in whom all the hopes of Israel were to be realized, cannot be seriously doubted. The very title " the Son of Man," as adopted by Jesus and freely applied to Himself as His favourite designation, involved, it is now generally recognized, Messianic assumptions (see Sanday, *Outlines of the Life of Christ*[2], Edinburgh, 1906, p. 92 ff., *The Life of Christ in Recent Research*, Oxford, 1907, p. 123 ff.). This claim He had already supported by His life and work. His miracles—works of God wrought through Him (cf. John xiv. 10)—were proofs of His mission as God's accredited messenger to Israel (Acts ii. 22, " a man accredited to you by God through miracles, wonders, and signs which God performed by him among you "; cf. Acts x. 38, " anointed of the Holy Ghost and with power he went about doing good, for God was with him "). This claim, however, was apparently contradicted and denied by His death on the Cross, which to the Jew was the symbol of Divine rejection (v. 30, x. 39). Through the Death on the Cross, therefore, the Jews' verdict on Jesus seemed Divinely supported. But through the Resurrection as not merely His being raised on the third day (Acts x. 40) but His being exalted to the right hand of God

in power and glory, Israel's act of rejection was Divinely
reversed, and the claim of Jesus to be the Christ was
for ever vindicated. " This Jesus has God raised up "
(Acts ii. 32). " The God of our fathers has glorified
Jesus his servant " (iii. 13 ; cf. ii. 33, v. 31, vii. 55).
" God has made him both Lord and Christ, this Jesus
whom ye crucified " (Acts ii. 36 ; cf. ix. 22). " Up-
lifted then by God's right hand, and receiving from the
Father the long-promised Holy Spirit, he has poured on
us what you now see and hear " (ii. 33 [Moffatt]).
There could be but one conclusion—earth's rejected was
God's accepted.

(*b*) Through the Resurrection the *Divinity* of Jesus
was established. He was shown to be not only Messiah
but the Son of God. A unique relation to God He had
Himself claimed. The title " Son of God," indeed, is
found only in the Fourth Gospel applied by Jesus to
Himself. In the Synoptics it is used to describe the impression made by Him upon others (*e.g.* on the possessed,
Mark iii. 11, v. 7, and parallel ; on the centurion, Mark
xv. 39 and parallel ; on the disciples, Matt. xiv. 33 ; on
the Baptist, John i. 34 ; on Nathanael, John i. 49). The
crowning instance is the confession of Peter, " Thou art
the Christ, the Son of the living God " (Matt. xvi. 16).
That on this matter of His Divine Sonship our Lord
maintained a great measure of reserve and reticence was
quite in keeping with His whole method of self-revelation. The truth of His Divine Sonship was not one
that could be taught the disciples as a dogma ; it must
be allowed to break naturally upon them as they increasingly divined the uniqueness of His character. But

we see in the records of the Evangelists how Jesus consistently sought to guide the thoughts of His disciples
concerning Himself into true and worthy lines.   He
uniformly claimed to stand in a unique relation to God.
He habitually speaks of God as " my Father " (Matt.
23 times), never embracing Himself with His disciples
as being in the same sense sons of God.   He speaks of
Himself as " the Son " in a unique sense (Matt. xi. 27 ;
Luke x. 22 ; Mark xiii. 32).   He attributes to Himself
powers and prerogatives which imply essential coequality
with God.   He claims perfect mutuality of understanding
as well as of will with the Father, whereby He possesses
an exclusive power of manifesting Him (Matt. xi. 27 ;
Luke x. 22).   He claims to do for men what only God
can do—to grant forgiveness (Matt. ix. 6 ; Mark ii. 10 ;
Luke v. 24) and to bestow the Holy Spirit (Matt. x. 19 ;
Luke xii. 12).   And, further, He demands from men
that complete surrender and utter devotion of life which
can be granted only to God (Matt. x. 37 ; Luke xiv. 26).
So it is altogether in keeping with the Synoptic representation when the Fourth Gospel records such sayings
as these : " I and the Father are one " (thing or essence,
ἕν) (x. 30), " He who has seen me has seen the Father "
(xiv. 9), " I am in the Father, and the Father is in me "
(xiv. 11), " the Jews sought the more to kill him because
he said, God was his peculiar (ἴδιον) Father, making
himself equal to God " (v. 18).

The claim of Jesus to be the Son of God is thus
implied in His attitude throughout, and for refusing to
disown it He was counted a blasphemer and condemned
to death (Matt. xxvi. 63, 65 f., xxvii. 43 ; cf. John x. 36).

Such a death — a "hanging on a gibbet"—seemed to be a confirmation of the judgment of His enemies, but the Resurrection was God's great declaration in action substantiating the truth of Jesus' claim : "declared Son of God with power according to the spirit of holiness by the resurrection of the dead" (Rom. i. 4). No blasphemer was He. The Resurrection "declared," defined, or marked Him out to be (ὁρισθέντος) what He always truly was—Son of God. For the Sonship thus declared "in power" (ἐν δυνάμει—no longer in humiliation but in power, the power of exalted Lordship) by the Resurrection was "according to" or answered to the spirit of holiness (κατὰ πνεῦμα ἁγιωσύνης), the spirit of exceptional and transcendent holiness which was the inmost reality in the person and life of Jesus, and testified to His peculiar relation to God. Divine Sonship, that is to say, was not an honour to which for the first time Christ was exalted after His death. The Resurrection only displayed Him as being what He was inalienably from the first, and installed Him in the dignity which corresponded to His nature. "In virtue of His resurrection . . . Christ is established in that dignity which is His and which answers to His nature" (Denney, *Expos. Gk. Test.*, on Rom. i. 4).

For St. Paul the conviction of the Divine Sonship of Jesus dated from the appearing to him on the way to Damascus of the Glorified Christ. What was revealed to him then was that the Crucified One was the Son of God in power. So that the gospel he immediately began to preach was "that Jesus is the Son of God" (Acts ix. 20). It is sometimes maintained that

the " Son of God " was a recognized title of the Messiah
(cf. *En.* cv. 2 ; *4 Ezra* vii. 28 f., xiii. 32, 37, 52, xiv. 9),
and that we cannot argue from the mere use of the
phrase to His Divinity. But it is not a case of thus
arguing. We have but to take the first writing of his
which has come down to us—1 Thess.—to see there
writ large what the assertion of the Divine Sonship of
Jesus meant for St. Paul. In this first extant New
Testament writing (written, according to Sanday, probably about A.D. 51, *i.e.* about twenty years after the
Resurrection) three remarkable predications are made of
Jesus :

(1) In the first verse, the Glorified Jesus is bracketed
in dignity with God the Father. St. Paul and his
companions give solemn greeting to " the Church of the
Thessalonians (which is) in God the Father and the
Lord Jesus Christ " (ver. 1). The wonder of such a
juxtaposition is realized only when we remember that
St. Paul was a strict Jew, in whose blood therefore
monotheism ran like a passion. Yet this Jewish apostle
does not scruple to place Jesus side by side with God,
and assume a like estimate of Him on the part of those
to whom he writes.

(2) In this brief letter Jesus is more than twenty
times referred to as " Lord " ($K\acute{v}\rho\iota o\varsigma$). The disciples
had been in the habit of addressing their Master as
" Lord " during His lifetime, using the term as a title of
authority in a sense not very different from that in
which any Rabbi might be addressed by his pupils
(John xiii. 13 f.) (see Sanday in Hastings' *Dict. of Bible*,
ii. 648[b]). But that sense is no longer adequate to the

apostolic usage; the word has become filled with a deeper meaning, being used as the LXX equivalent of the Old Testament "Jahweh" and as signifying Divine power and sovereignty. What Jahweh was to Israel, that Jesus was to the religious consciousness of St. Paul —the One who has earned the place of Sovereign in his heart, and whom he feels constrained to worship and serve.

(3) Prayer is addressed to Jesus directly, and not merely offered in His name—"Now may our God and Father himself, and our Lord Jesus, direct our way unto you" (iii. 11). And all this, it is significant to note, is referred to by the Apostle only in the passing, without the slightest indication that it was a novel or unfamiliar attitude to his readers. In his subsequent Epistles St. Paul gives fuller and more developed doctrinal expression to his conviction of the truth of the Divine Sonship of Jesus. Personal pre-existence in the Godhead is unambiguously affirmed of Him in 2 Cor. viii. 9 ("ye know the grace of our Lord Jesus Christ," etc.) and in Phil. ii. 6 ff. ("though he was divine by nature, he did not snatch at equality with God but emptied himself by taking the nature of a servant," etc. [Moffatt]). In Col. i. 15–20 His cosmic significance is dwelt upon. As "the image (εἰκών) of the invisible God," He occupies a position of unique pre-eminence and sovereignty, and is agent or mediator and end in creation as well as in redemptive history ("in him were all things created . . . all things have been created through him, and with a view to [εἰς] him"; cf. 1 Cor. viii. 6, x. 4). But already in his earliest as truly as in his latest writings full,

eternal, essential Divinity is ascribed to Jesus as Son of God, whereby He is placed alongside the Father in honour and worship.

St. Paul's use of the term " Son of God " in this transcendent sense has been traced to Hellenistic influence. While the title had been employed by the earliest Christian community " in a very harmless sense," St. Paul gave it the altogether new and mythical sense of a God who had descended from heaven, a sense which was intelligible enough to Greeks and heathen but not to Jews with their strict monotheism ; and in so doing he " became the creator of the new Christology, which drew its inspiration, not from history, but from something above it—from a mythical being, and which won over the heathen for this very reason " (Wernle, *Beginnings of Christianity*, Eng. tr., 2 vols., London, 1903–04, i. 250). "Son of God," as employed by St. Paul, is thus held to be primarily a Gentile title, one which was sometimes applied to the Emperors, like the title " Lord " (*e.g.* it is so found in a letter of the Emperor Augustus dated A.D. 5 ; see *Expositor*, 6th ser., vii. [1903] 114, and Knowling, *Testimony of St. Paul*, p. 44). This Imperial usage, Deissmann conjectures, may have first suggested to St. Paul the application of the title to Jesus (*Bibelstudien*, Marburg, 1895, i. 167, Eng. tr., *Bible Studies*, Edinburgh, 1901, p. 166 f.). But " Son of God," if a Gentile, was also a Jewish title, and, as Knowling points out, it is most significant that the first and earliest intimation which we have in Acts of St. Paul's Christian teaching is this, that " in the synagogues " —not to Greeks or Romans, but to Jews and proselytes

—" he proclaimed Jesus, that he is the Son of God "
(ix. 20).

If St. Paul had interpreted " Son of God " differently
from the other apostles, and if the deification of Christ
had been due to him, the surprising thing is that we do
not hear of any opposition on this point between him
and the older apostles.   The older apostles and St. Paul
differed no doubt in many things, but there is no trace
that they differed in the estimate which they formed of
the Person of Christ, and of His relationship to the
Father.   St. Paul's representation of Christ is only a
more developed expression of what is present already in
solution in the primitive apostolic teaching.   Of this St.
Peter's sermons in Acts and his First Epistle may be
taken as representative.

In St. Peter's sermons in Acts, while no attempt is
made at a fully developed doctrine of the Person of
Christ, He is quite definitely placed on the side of God
as over against man, the theme of the gospel and the
object of faith.   Through His resurrection and exaltation Jesus is proclaimed not only " Messiah " (iii. 18–20,
iv. 25–28), but "giver of the Holy Spirit" (ii. 23),
" Prince of life " (iii. 15, v. 31), " Saviour " (iv. 12,
v. 21), and " Judge of living and dead " (x. 42, a pre-
rogative which in the Old Testament belongs to God
and to God alone).   Prayer is offered to Him directly
(i. 24, vii. 59), so that one mode of describing Christians
in these early days was to speak of them as those that
called upon the name of Jesus (ix. 21).   And already in
his first sermon we find St. Peter applying to Christ the
term "Lord" (Κύριος, Acts ii. 21, 33, 36; cf. iii. 13,

21, v. 31, x. 36), the same term as is used of Jahweh in the LXX, thus assigning to Him Divine sovereignty and authority. The mere use of the word Κύριος may not in itself necessarily involve Divinity. The Jews applied it to their Messiah (Mark xii. 36 f. and parallels) without thereby, it is said, pronouncing him to be God. But, as Knowling points out, " it is not merely that the early Christians addressed their Ascended Lord so many times by the same name which is used of Jehovah in the LXX . . . but that they did not hesitate to refer to Him the attributes and the prophecies which the great prophets of the Jewish nation had associated with the name of Jehovah " (*Expos. Gk. Test.*, on Acts ii. 21).

In his First Epistle St. Peter represents the same point of view in slightly fuller and more developed form. The Spirit of God is definitely spoken of as " the Spirit of Christ " (i. 11) ; and although the title " Son of God " is not employed, we find the expression " the God and Father of our Lord Jesus Christ " (i. 3), with an undeniable implication of Christ's special Sonship. Christians are called to " sanctify in their hearts Christ as Lord " (iii. 15) in words which in the Old Testament are applied to Jahweh and His sanctification by Israel (Isa. viii. 13). He is proclaimed to be Lord not only of the spiritual world but of the material as related to and subserving the spiritual, " angels and authorities and powers being made subject unto him " (1 Pet. iii. 22). It is a disputed question whether i. 11 and i. 20 do or do not imply the real pre-existence of Christ. While the language of the former seems satisfied if we take it to mean simply that the Divine Spirit, now so bound up

8

with Christ that it can be called *His* Spirit, moved also
in the prophets of old, the latter passage is more significant.   "While the word 'foreknown' (προεγνωσμένου)
in no way involves the pre-existence of Christ, since it
is used even of Christians in i. 2, yet the unusual combination of 'foreknown' with 'manifested' may justly be
considered as placing the matter beyond doubt.   Only
that can be manifested which was in being before
manifestation" (H. R. Mackintosh, *The Person of
Jesus Christ*, Edinburgh, 1912, p. 45 f.).   With the
sermons of St. Peter in Acts and his First Epistle as
representing the general conception of Christ current
in the earliest Apostolic Age may be coupled the
Epistle of St. James, where Jesus is extolled as "the
Lord of glory" (ii. 1) and ranked with God in honour
and dignity" (i. 1); and the brief Epistle of Jude,
who describes Jesus as "our only Master and Lord,
Jesus Christ" (ver. 4), whose "slave" (δοῦλος) he is
(ver. 1).

As representing the more developed apostolic doctrine,
we have not only the Epistles of St. Paul but the Epistle
to the Hebrews and the Johannine writings.   In
Hebrews the central thought is that of the Divine Sonship of Christ, in virtue of which He is the Mediator of
the new and better covenant (xii. 24, ix. 15, viii. 6).
He is announced as a "Son" (i. 2), transcendently related
to God, the effulgence of the Father's glory and the very
image of His substance (i. 3), creator, upholder, and heir
of all things (i. 2, 10), who, though thus eternal and
Divine, because the children were partakers of flesh and
blood, Himself likewise partook of the same and is now

through His suffering and sacrifice exalted at the right
hand of the majesty on high (i. 3, viii. 1, x. 5).   In the
Fourth Gospel the emphasis on the Divine Sonship is
marked throughout, so that even such a critic as J.
Weiss admits that in this Gospel Christ is God in the
fullest sense, possessing "those qualities which constitute the nature of the Deity" (*Christ: The Beginnings of
Dogma*, Eng. tr., London, 1911, p. 148 ff.).   The view
of the writer is summed up in the Prologue in terms
of the rebaptized Logos conception of which he predi-
cates His eternity ("existed in the very beginning,"
ver. 1 [Moffatt]), His eternal personal relation to God
(" was with [πρός] God," ver. 1 ; "was with God in the
very beginning," ver. 2), His agency in creation (" through
him all existence came into being, no existence came into
being apart from him," ver. 3), giver of life and light to
the whole race of mankind, the medium alike of creation
and of revelation (" in him life lay, and this life was the
Light for men," ver. 4 ; "the real Light which lightens
every man," ver. 9).   In 1 John such a unity between
God and the Son is recognized that he who confesses the
Son hath the Father also (v. 20).   In the Apocalypse
Christ is represented as He whom all creation unites to
worship as it worships God Almighty (i. 6 ; cf. vii. 12).
God and the Lamb receive united adoration (v. 13, vii.
10).   He is the "First and the Last," the "Beginning
and the End" (i. 8, xxi. 6, xxii. 13), the Lord of the
churches, who holds their stars or guardian angels in
His hand (i. 16, 20), who is Ruler of the nations and
King of kings, the all-wise and almighty Judge of the
nations (vii. 9, xv. 4).

2. *Evidential with regard to His Work, especially His Death*

The Resurrection was not only the confirmation of Christ's claim to Sonship and Messiahship; it was through this the Divine justification of Jesus' claim as to the redemptive character of His life and work as culminating in His death, and the public declaration of its acceptance. The Messiah was looked for as coming in outward glory, but Jesus came in a way that was the very opposite of this. His life on earth had been one of humiliation and suffering, of self-denying service and sacrifice for others, until at last the culminating point of His sacrifice was reached in His death. All were "offended" in Him. He needed to be justified, and the Resurrection was His Divine justification or vindication. In the Epistle to the Philippians His resurrection (and exaltation) is connected with His "making himself of no reputation" and taking upon Him the form of a servant (ii. 6–11). In Romans (i. 4) it is in contrast with His having been made of the seed of David according to the flesh that He is said to have been declared Son of God with power. Above all, His death needed justification. Jesus had Himself while on earth proclaimed the necessity of His suffering and death. But this was so contrary to Jewish conceptions of the Messiah that the first disciples had difficulty in attaining to it. "The idea of the Messianic sufferings and death is one that wakes no echo in the heart of any Jewish contemporary of our Lord, not excepting even His disciples" (L. A. Muirhead, *Eschatology of Jesus,* London, 1904, p. 206), and the Death on the Cross when it came was fatal, in Jewish eyes, to Messianic claims. This was the great σκάνδαλον. It was His resurrection, and the fact that by it He had been " declared " the Son of God with power, that showed the peculiarity and importance of His death. So St. Paul represents the case. If Jesus was indeed both Lord and Christ, as through his experience on the Damascus road he had come to know, the death which He died could not be what it seemed to be, a curse, the death of a malefactor and blasphemer, but a Divine appointment for the salvation of men. There must be in it a Divine virtue. " God was in Christ," even Christ the crucified, reconciling the world unto Himself (2 Cor. v. 19 ; cf. 1 Cor. xv. 17 ; Rom. iv. 25, vi. 4–7). It was a vicarious death ; He was delivered up for our transgressions (Rom. iv. 25), and the Resurrection was the assurance that God had accepted Christ's atoning work, and that the foundation of perfect reconciliation between God and man had been laid. In the light of the revelation of the Resurrection, the Death on the Cross lost its shame and became a spring of blessing, the central " commendation " or proof of Divine love (Rom. v. 8).

Already in the primitive Christian community, following hints of our Lord Himself in His earthly and then in His post-Resurrection teaching, we have the atoning significance of the Death represented. That Jesus " died for our sins according to the Scriptures "—not only the fact of the Death but its atoning significance—was part of the tradition which St. Paul had received and which, he claimed, was common to himself and the older apostles (1 Cor. xv. 3, 11). " The inference," Weizsäcker acknowledges, "is indisputable; the primitive Church already taught, and proved from Scripture, that the death of Jesus exerted a saving influence in the forgiveness of sin" (*Apost. Age*[2], i. 130 f.).

This is borne out by the reports of St. Peter's speeches in the Acts, where the death of Jesus is represented as a Divine necessity, taking place " by the determined counsel and foreknowledge of God" (ii. 23; cf. iv. 28), and as in accordance with prophecy (iii. 18; cf. Christ's post-Resurrection teaching, Luke xxiv. 2.   Isa. liii. seems to have been the special message in the Apostle's mind—the Suffering Messiah being frequently identified in these early speeches with the Servant of the Lord in Isaiah, *e.g.* iii. 13, iv. 27; cf. viii. 35).   So, although represented as a crime on the part of the Jews (ii. 23, iii. 13–15, v. 30), the death of Jesus is viewed as a fact Divinely foreordained and Divinely necessary.   This Divine necessity of the Death has reference to its saving or redemptive significance in virtue of which the great blessing of the gospel, offered in the name of Jesus, is the forgiveness of sins (ii. 38, iii. 19, v. 31, x. 43).   In these early sermons or discourses the redemptive significance of the Death is not developed.   We have to remember that " the Petrine speeches in the Acts were called forth by special circumstances and (except the speeches recorded in Acts x. 30–43, xv. 7–11) were all addressed to non-Christian Jews at Jerusalem.   We have no right, therefore, to look to them for the full cycle of Christian doctrine which even in the beginning of the Gospel Peter had apprehended " (Chase, Hastings' *Dict. of Bible*, iii. 793[b]).   In the First Epistle of Peter we have a somewhat more developed doctrine; the atoning efficacy of the suffering and death of Christ being described in varied language—covenant blood (i. 2), ransom (i. 18 f.), sin-bearing (ii. 20 ff.), substitution, the sacrifice of the righteous for the unrighteous (iii. 18).

In St. Paul the redemptive significance of the Death is further developed. He died "for our sins" (1 Cor. xv. 3; 2 Cor. v. 21); a "ransom" (λύτρον, 1 Tim. ii. 6); through His death there is inaugurated a New Covenant (1 Cor. xi. 28), in which the Divine purpose of "salvation" is realized: deliverance from wrath (Rom. v. 9), from the curse of the Law (Gal. iii. 13), and the imparting of eternal life (1 Thess. v. 9 f.). The shedding of His blood was a sacrifice which had propitiatory value (Rom. iii. 25 f., v. 9; 1 Cor. v. 9), in virtue of which men are brought into a new relation to God, treated as righteous (Rom. iii. 24), "accepted in the Beloved" (Eph. i. 6). This sacrificial significance of the Death is specially emphasized by the writer to the Hebrews, who finds in the sacrifices of the Old Covenant types and shadows of the sacrifice of Christ. Through its propitiatory efficacy the Death is viewed as a crown of glory (ii. 9; cf. v. 8 f.). In the Johannine writings "Jesus Christ the righteous" is represented as "the propitiation for our sins" (1 John ii. 2, iv. 10; cf. Rev. i. 5, v. 6, 9, 12), in the Gospel the suffering and death being viewed, as in Heb., as a glorification (xiii. 31). "He [St. John] . . . does not ever, like St. Paul (e.g. Phil. ii. 8, 9), separate it [the Passion] as a crisis of humiliation from the glory which followed" (Westcott, on John xii. 32; cf. Milligan, *Resurrection*, p. 314).

3. *Evidential with regard to Man's Eternal Destiny*

Another aspect of the evidential significance of the resurrection of Christ for the Apostolic Church is that which concerns the eternal destiny of those " who through him do believe in God." Already in the Old Testament we have foreshadowings of the belief in a continued personal life with God after death. The religious relation of the soul to God was felt to carry with it the pledge of such a continued life. Fellowship with God constitutes a bond which death cannot sever. " Immortality is the corollary of religion. If there be religion, that is, if God be, there is immortality " (Davidson, *Job*, Cambridge, 1884, p. 296). As Jesus Himself put it, interpreting and supporting this fundamental Old Testament source of the faith in immortality, God is " not a God of dead people but of living " (Matt. xxii. 32 ; Mark xii. 27 ; Luke xx. 38). And this immortality was for the Hebrew an immortality of the whole personal being of man, body as well as soul. The conception of a disembodied future life was entirely foreign to the Old Testament—belonging to ethnic not to Hebrew thought. Such a destiny, indeed, could be for the Old Testament believer but a hope, a faith, a faith venture, though involved in the very nature of religion as fellowship with God. If certainty, if assured confidence of such a full personal immortality, was to be attained, some more " sure word " of God must be spoken ; and such a sure word the Apostolic Church found in the resurrection of Jesus. As the crowning example of a life lived in fellowship with God, and trusting God for the future, Jesus supplied the test case, the crucial instance, of God's love.

Since therefore Jesus—the man Jesus—was raised from the grave, the faith in the Resurrection grounded in the life of fellowship with God has received its final seal and assurance. The resurrection of those who are His is guaranteed—" For if we believe that Jesus died and rose again, even so them also that are fallen asleep in Jesus will God bring with him" (1 Thess. iv. 14). The empty grave therefore, as Harnack admits with some inconsequence, is "the birthplace of the indestructible belief that death is vanquished, that there is a life eternal" (*What is Christianity*?[3], p. 165).

St. Paul puts this evidential significance of the Resurrection first negatively : "If Christ be not risen, then they also which have fallen asleep in Christ have perished ($\dot{a}\pi\dot{\omega}\lambda o\nu\tau o$)" (1 Cor. xv. 18). They have "perished" not in the sense of suffering annihilation or extinction of conscious existence, but of undergoing deprivation of continued existence in any sense in which it is worth having—deprivation of "life" through separation from God, the Sheol state of existence. (For St. Paul's use of $\dot{a}\pi\dot{o}\lambda\lambda\upsilon\sigma\theta a\iota$ and $\dot{a}\pi\dot{\omega}\lambda\epsilon\iota a$ as the antithesis of $\sigma\dot{\omega}\zeta\epsilon\sigma\theta a\iota$ and $\sigma\omega\tau\eta\rho\dot{\iota}a$ see Kennedy, *St. Paul's Conceptions of the Last Things*, p. 119 ff.) "But now hath Christ been raised and become the first fruits ($\dot{a}\pi a\rho\chi\dot{\eta}$) of them that are asleep" (ver. 20). This is the more positive statement of it. As the first ripe sheaf is the earnest and guarantee of the coming harvest, so the resurrection of Christ is the pledge and guarantee of the resurrection of those who are His (cf. Col. i. 18 ; Rev. i. 5, $\pi\rho\omega\tau\dot{o}\tau o\kappa o\varsigma$ $\dot{\epsilon}\kappa$

τῶν νεκρῶν, " the first born from the dead "). So St.
Peter speaks of Christians being " born anew to a life of
hope through the resurrection of Jesus Christ from the
dead, born to an unscathed, inviolate unfading inherit-
ance " (1 Pet. i. 3 f. [Moffatt]).

But more, the resurrection of Christ is not only the
assurance or pledge of the full personal immortality of
believers ; it is also the revelation of the nature of this
immortal life. It " has brought life and immortality to
light " (2 Tim. i. 10); it has displayed it to our view.
He has risen in possession of a body like ours, only
glorified and made free from the law of sin and death, a
body " spiritual " in the sense of being the perfect instrument of the purposes of spirit. In this glorified embodied
state of the Risen Christ we have a look at the nature of
the future state of believers. At present we are pent up
in a body which is but an imperfect medium of our will
or spirit. It is " a body of death " (Rom. vii. 24), full
of weakness and corruption, limiting our powers of
service. But " this body that belongs to our low estate "
shall be transformed " till it resembles the body of his
Glory " (Phil. iii. 21 [Moffatt]). For " if the Spirit of
him that raised up Jesus from the dead dwelleth in you,
he that raised up Christ Jesus from the dead shall
quicken also your mortal bodies through his Spirit that
dwelleth in you " (Rom. viii. 11). (On the nature of
the Christian's resurrection-body and the connexion
between the resurrection of Christ and the resurrection of
believers, whereby the former is not only the pledge or
guarantee but the ground of the latter, see, more fully,
below, p. 141 ff.).

CHAPTER VIII

THE SIGNIFICANCE OF THE RESURRECTION OF CHRIST FOR APOSTOLIC CHRISTIANITY (*Continued*)

II. Essential or Constitutive Significance

THE evidential significance of the resurrection of Christ for Apostolic Christianity has now been considered, but the heart of the apostolic representation is not reached until it is perceived that the Resurrection is not simply an external seal or evidential appendage added on to guarantee certain truths about Christ and His work, but an essential or constitutive element in the work itself, an integral part of His redemptive revelation. Such a view as that of Herrmann already referred to, which lays the chief stress on the impression produced by Christ's life, making the Resurrection at most a deduction of faith without vital relation to redemption, fails to do justice to the inner meaning of the fact. This more inner vital significance of the Resurrection for apostolic thought and life as the necessary sequel of the Incarnation and Crucifixion, and essential to the completion of the work of redemption, may be presented under the following heads:

1. *What it meant for Christ Himself*

The Resurrection was essential to Christian faith, because of what it meant for Christ Himself. As the transition from a state of humiliation to a state of exaltation, the entrance in His risen manhood on a new life of exalted power and sovereignty, whereby He became Lord over all, the Resurrection formed a new beginning in the life of Christ Himself.   This is the central significance of the Resurrection insisted on by St. Peter in his sermons recorded in Acts: "God hath made him both Lord (*Κύριον*) and Christ, this Jesus whom ye crucified" (ii. 36); "Him hath God exalted at his right hand to be a Prince and a Saviour" (v. 31); "therefore being by the right hand of God exalted . . . he hath poured forth this" (ii. 33), and the healing of the lame man is pointed to as further evidence of His exalted sovereignty (iv. 10). *Κύριος*, the LXX name for Jahweh and the characteristic apostolic title for the Exalted Jesus, defines Him as One who is sovereign in the spheres both of grace and of nature, Lord not only over the Church but over all creation.   This too is the connotation or significance of the phrase "at the right hand of God"—a phrase borrowed from Ps. cx. 1 and oftener used in the New Testament than any other words of the Old Testament. It defines Christ's exaltation as a sharing in the universal sovereignty and almighty power of God.   So in 1 Pet. iii. 22 the statement that "angels and authorities and powers" are "made subject unto him" is the affirmation of His personal participation in the universal sovereignty of God, whose servants the angels and authorities and powers are.

This is most strikingly expressed by St. Paul, for whom the greatness of the Resurrection, as the supreme manifestation of Divine power ("the surpassing greatness of his power," Eph. i. 19 [Moffatt]), consisted in the fact that it was not merely the raising of Jesus from the dead, but His exaltation and enthronement " in the heavenly sphere (ἐν τοῖς ἐπουρανίοις) . . . the sphere of spiritual activities . . ., which lies behind the world of sense, . . . the sphere of all the ruling forces of the universe " (J. Armitage Robinson, *St. Paul's Epistle to the Ephesians*, London, 1903, p. 20 f.), " above all the angelic Rulers, Authorities, Powers, and Lords " — above all powers whether of the natural sphere or of the spiritual —and all this for redemptive ends, that He might be " head over everything for the church, the church which is his Body " (Eph. i. 20–22 [Moffatt]). As he puts it in the Epistle to the Philippians, " God raised him high and conferred on him a Name above all names [Κύριος], so that before the Name of Jesus every knee should bend in heaven, on earth, and underneath the earth, and every tongue confess that ' Jesus Christ is Lord,' to the glory of God the Father " (ii. 9–11 [Moffatt]). The Resurrection thus constituted a " crisis " in the experience of Christ Himself. Through it His activity was raised to a new level, whereby He became clothed with absolute might to carry out the issues of His saving work on earth.

The frequency with which St. Paul speaks of Jesus as " Lord " (Κύριος) is remarkable. The word occurs some 131 times in his writings (see Feine, *Theol. des NT*, p. 344). In his first Epistle, 1 Thess., the title is applied to the Risen Christ more than 20 times. The peculiar significance of St. Paul's use of the term is sometimes minimized on the ground that it was used in ancient times to express the relation of a king to his subjects—cf. Acts xxv. 26, where it is applied to the Roman Emperor—and in Oriental religions to express the relation between a god and his worshippers.   So Deissmann maintains that the Pauline title "the Lord" is "a genuinely Oriental predicate," and that St. Paul uses it as a silent protest against the acknowledgment of any other Lord, even the Roman Emperor, as a rival to the Lordship of Christ (see Feine, *Jesus Christus und Paulus*, p. 38).   So Heitmüller and Bousset claim that St. Paul's view of Jesus as Κύριος was determined by the Hellenistic Christianity which he found in Damascus and Antioch.   But if it was a Gentile it was also a Jewish title, being the LXX name for Jahweh, and this for St. Paul as a Jew was its nearer context.   And St. Paul's application of the term to the Exalted Jesus was in line with the usage of the early Christian community (see above, pp 112 f., 124).   To say, as Pfleiderer does, that the common faith of St. Paul and the early disciples in Jesus as Lord was due to a pre-Christian conception of Messiah which came ultimately from Oriental sources, is to cut it off from its origin in apostolic experience and to leave unexplained what is the central and essential fact to be explained—how Lordship came to be predicated of One who died on a Cross of shame.

When we ask in what ways the Risen Lord exercises His sovereignty and power, we find the apostolic writers dwelling especially upon two manifestations of it: (*a*) the giving of the Holy Spirit, and (*b*) the intercession of Christ at the Father's right hand.

(*a*) The giving of the Spirit is represented by the apostles as the gift of the Exalted Lord by which He carries on His work on earth, and secures the ends for which He lived and died.   "Being therefore by the right hand of God exalted," says St. Peter, connecting the fact with the exaltation of Christ, "and having received from the Father the promise of the Holy Spirit, he has poured forth on us what you now see and hear" (Acts ii. 33).   So intimately was the giving of the Spirit connected with the exaltation and glorification of Christ that St. John can say that there was no gift of the Spirit before the Ascension.   "Spirit was not yet, because

Jesus was not yet glorified" (John vii. 39). He was anointed with the Holy Spirit Himself, and by the power of the Spirit accomplished the work given Him to do; but not till His work on earth was done and His glory entered did He possess the Spirit in such wise as to be able to bestow it on men. It was the promise of the Father—part of Christ's reward for His work on earth —and, as such, a sure proof of God's acceptance of that work.

Thus it is that the characteristic apostolic name for the Spirit is "the Spirit of Christ" or "the Spirit of the Lord [Jesus]" (Acts xvi. 7, R.V.; Rom. viii. 9; 2 Cor. iii. 17; Gal. iv. 6; Phil. i. 19; 1 Pet. i. 11), not only as having dwelt in Christ Himself, but as being the gift of Christ as Christ was the gift of the Father (cf. John xiv. 26, xv. 26). Further, the Spirit is called the Spirit of Christ as having Christ for His theme, His office being to witness to, interpret, and glorify Christ, and thus carry on His work on earth (cf. John xv. 26 f., xvi. 14). As such the Spirit is characterized chiefly in three ways: (1) as the Spirit of *truth*, to lead men into the truth as it is in Jesus, to take of the things of Christ and show us their meaning (John xiv. 26, xv. 26, xvi. 13 f.; Acts ii. 4, vi. 10 *et passim*; 1 Cor. ii. 10, xii. 3, etc.); (2) as the Spirit of *holiness*, to convince of sin, of righteousness, and of judgment (John xvi. 8), to help our infirmities (Rom. viii. 26), to set free from the power of sin and death (Rom. viii. 2, 10, 13; Gal. v. 25, etc.), to produce the virtues of the Christian character which are the fruit of the Spirit (Gal. v. 22; Eph. v. 9), and to conform us in body and in spirit into the likeness of the

Risen Christ (Rom. viii. 29 f., x. 13 ; 1 Cor. iii. 16, vi. 19, xv. 42–44 ; 2 Cor. iii. 18 ; Gal. ii. 20, etc.) ; (3) as the Spirit of *power*, to enable men to be effective witnesses in word and life to the Risen Christ (Acts i. 8, iii. 12, iv. 7, etc.).

The function of the Spirit was thus to realize a new kind of fellowship between Christ and His followers—a spiritual fellowship with a living, everywhere present Lord—in and through which they were led into truth and holiness and power. The coming of the Spirit, therefore, is not to be looked upon as a compensation or substitute for an absent Christ ; it is the higher mode of Christ's own presence, to which He pointed forward when He said, " I will be with you all the time, to the very end of the world " (Matt. xxviii. 20). On Christ's own lips, the promise " the Comforter will come " is interchangeable with " I will come to you " (John xiv. 18, xv. 26).

St. Paul in more than one passage expressly identifies the Risen Christ with the Spirit (*e.g.* 2 Cor. iii. 17, " the Lord is the Spirit," and ver. 18, " we are changed into the same image by the Lord the Spirit "). And on this ground it is sometimes argued that for St. Paul the Risen Exalted Christ and the Spirit are really one and the same (*e.g.* von Dobschütz, *Ostern und Pfingsten*, p. 34). To identify the Risen Lord and the Spirit, however, without qualification in the face of the threefold benediction in the same Epistle (xiii. 14) is unwarranted. What St. Paul meant was that between the Spirit and the power of the Risen Christ no experimental distinction could be made. " The truth of the passage is

the same as that of Rom. viii. 9 ff. : 'If any man have
not *the Spirit of Christ* he is none of his.   And if *Christ
is in you,*' etc.   Here, so far as the practical experience of
Christians goes, no distinction is made between the Spirit
of Christ and Christ Himself ; Christ dwells in Christians
through His Spirit " (Denney, *Expositor's Bible*, " 2 Cor.,"
p. 134 ; cf. same writer's *Christian Doct. of Reconciliation,*
p. 311 f.).   " What we learn from his (St. Paul's) utter-
ances is, that, to the Christian consciousness, Christ and
the Spirit of God are one and the same, that the influence
of the Personal Christ upon us is equivalent, as regards
its moral and religious effects, to the energy of the
Divine Spirit, and that it is only through our connexion
with His Person and our faith in Him that we experience
that specific working of God's Spirit that was exemplified
supremely in His life " (Somerville, *St. Paul's Conception
of Christ,* p. 120).   " What the Apostle means by his
form of verbal identification [' the Lord is the Spirit '] is
rather the religious certainty that Jesus Christ, in whom
God redeems men, and the Spirit, in whom He communi-
cates Himself to men, are so indissolubly bound up in
one, act so absolutely for the same end and through the
same means, and from the standpoint of the practical
issue they are seen as merged in each other.   They are
one as the fountain and the stream are one.   ' Christ in
you, or the Spirit of Christ in you ; these are not different
realities ; but the one is the method of the other '
(Moberly) " (H. R. Mackintosh in Hastings' Smaller *Dict.
of Bible,* p. 708[b] ; cf. the same writer's *The Person of
Jesus Christ,* p. 374).

(*b*) While thus through the Spirit the Exalted Christ

9

carries on His work on earth, by His intercession at the Father's right hand He Himself carries on His work in heaven. This aspect of the Risen Christ's activity is specially emphasized in the Epistle to the Hebrews, where it is represented as the culmination of His high-priestly functions, the entering "through his own blood," *i.e.* with the virtue of His atoning sacrifice in Him, into the holiest of all "to appear in the presence of God for us" (Heb. ix. 24), and the guarantee of the full effectiveness of His redemptive work, "wherefore also he is able to save to the uttermost them that draw near unto God through him, seeing he ever liveth to make intercession ($\dot{\epsilon}\nu\tau\nu\gamma\chi\acute{a}\nu\epsilon\iota\nu$) for them" (vii. 25). But in the other apostolic writings, both Pauline and Johannine, His intercession at God's right hand is equally represented as the culminating aspect of Christ's work, and "with a kind of adoring awe which is quite peculiar even in the New Testament" (Denney, *Studies in Theology*, London, 1894, p. 162). "It is Christ Jesus that died, yea rather, that was raised from the dead, who is at the right hand of God, who also maketh intercession ($\dot{\epsilon}\nu\tau\nu\gamma\chi\acute{a}\nu\epsilon\iota$) for us" (Rom. viii. 34, "who actually pleads for us" [Moffatt]). "These things write I unto you that ye sin not. And if any man sin, we have an advocate with the Father, Jesus Christ the righteous" (1 John ii. 1).

It would no doubt be misleading to represent His heavenly intercession as oral or vocal, as taking place in words or spoken entreaty. "Words imply distance and duality of a kind incongruous with the identity of life subsisting between Christ and the Father. Theirs is a unity that needs no language" (Mackintosh, *The Person of Jesus Christ*, p. 377). When the apostles speak of His "making intercession for us," they are not speaking of "specific acts done or words spoken by Christ in His glory. His glorified presence is an eternal presentation ; He pleads by what He is " (R. C. Moberly, *Ministerial Priesthood*, London, 1897, p. 246). On the other hand, it would seem to be doing less than justice to the apostolic thought to represent His intercession as nothing more than His appearance and constant presence before God for us, with the virtue of His atoning life and death in Him, God being thus continually reminded, as it were, at once of the efficacy of Christ's atoning work and of the needs of humanity. Apparently we should interpret the apostolic language (*e.g.* Heb. iv. 16, "that we may find grace to help in time of need," grace for timely succour) as implying that the intercession of Christ is not a continuous unvarying representation to God on behalf of men on the part of the Exalted Christ, but an intercession which relates itself sympathetically to the varying needs and exigencies of the believer's life.

This direct personal representation to God on our behalf is not to be conceived as limited to prayer. The verb ἐντυγχάνειν, translated " intercede," means to deal or transact with one person for another, and, when it stands alone without any limiting expressions, ought to be understood in a much wider sense than petition or prayer, viz. as "including the whole series of transactions in which one person may engage with another on behalf of a third " (Milligan, *The Ascension and Heavenly Priest-hood of our Lord*, p. 151). Christ's intercession is the

whole action or transaction in the presence of God of the
Exalted Christ, whereby, on the ground of His atoning
work, the full blessings of salvation are made over to
those "who come to God through him" (Heb. vii. 25 ;
cf. Rom. viii. 34).

2. *What it meant for Humanity*

In virtue of its being thus the entrance on a new life
of exalted power and Lordship in which He exercises
His full redemptive activity, the resurrection of Jesus
constitutes a new beginning in the life of humanity,
ushering in a new creative epoch. The Risen Jesus
becomes a new life-principle in men, a "life-creating
Spirit" (1 Cor. xv. 45, πνεῦμα ζωοποιοῦν) introducing
men into a new world of spiritual experience. This
epochal significance of the Resurrection St. Paul represents
by saying that in and by His resurrection Christ became
the "second Adam," the Founder and Head of a new
humanity, so that the resurrection of Christ represents as
real a crisis in the history of man as his creation
(Rom. v. 12 f. ; 1 Cor. xv. 45 ff.). "The first Adam
became a living soul" (1 Cor. xv. 45, ψυχὴ ζῶσα, a
person possessing a principle of life)—this marks the
crisis of man's creation. "The second Adam became a
life-creating spirit" (*ib.*)—this marks the crisis of man's
redemption whereby he becomes a "new creation" (καινὴ
κτίσις) and henceforth walks "in newness of life"
(Rom. vi. 4, ἐν καινότητι ζωῆς).

This new life into which believers are introduced
through union by faith with the living Lord St. Paul can
describe only by saying that he possesses the Spirit

($\pi\nu\epsilon\hat{v}\mu a$) of Jesus Christ (Rom. ix. 9), that the Spirit of Christ or the Spirit of God mediated through the Exalted Christ dwells in him (ix. 11) or that Christ lives in him, so that he can say, "I live; and yet no longer I, but Christ liveth in me" (Gal. ii. 20; cf. Rom. viii. 9–11). The life He now lives as a human being has, as its central determining principle, not himself but Christ. Christ is "our life" (Col. iii. 4, $\dot{\eta}$ $\zeta\omega\dot{\eta}$ $\dot{\eta}\mu\hat{\omega}\nu$). The $\zeta\omega\dot{\eta}$ of the believer is the very $\zeta\omega\dot{\eta}$ of the Exalted Christ (cf. Rom. viii. 10; 2 Cor. iv. 10 f.). Christianity for St. Paul is the condition of being "in Christ" ($\dot{\epsilon}\nu$ $X\rho\iota\sigma\tau\hat{\omega}$). A man "in Christ"—that is his definition of a Christian. The new dispensation or epoch inaugurated by the Resurrection and Exaltation is the dispensation of the Spirit predicted by Christ Himself (John xiv. 16, 26, xv. 26, xvi. 7).

By those who, like Pfleiderer and Beyschlag, trace St. Paul's view of Christ as "the second Adam," the man "from heaven" (1 Cor. xv. 47), to the influence of Philo's Jewish-Hellenic conception of a pre-existent heavenly Man, the *Urmensch* or archetypal model of man's creation, St. Paul is represented as conceiving of Christ in His pre-incarnate state merely as Man in heaven, the prototype of humanity (see J. Weiss, on 1 Cor. xv. 47, and Feine, *Theol. des NT*, p. 353). Even if we assume, however, that St. Paul borrowed the contrast in the first place from current Hellenic thought, using the *schema* lying to his hand, he filled it with a content determined not by the speculations of Alexandrian philosophy but by his own experience of the Risen Christ. He seems, indeed, expressly to contrast his own point of view with that of Philo, by designating the man "from heaven" not the "First Man" as in Philo, but the "Second Man." "That is not first which is spiritual but that which is natural" (1 Cor. xv. 46). It is only at His resurrection that Christ is represented by St. Paul as becoming the "second Adam," the life-giving head of a new humanity.

For the apostles, accordingly, *Christian life and experience in all its forms depends upon the Resurrection.*

(*a*) Our *justification* depends upon it. The great passage here is Rom. iv. 25 : "He was delivered up for our trespasses (διὰ τὰ παραπτώματα ἡμῶν) and was raised for our justification (διὰ τὴν δικαίωσιν ἡμῶν)." The latter clause is sometimes taken to mean that the Resurrection is necessary to our justification in the sense of being the great proof that the sacrifice of the Death was Divinely accepted, thus evoking faith in us. "He was delivered up [to death] because of our trespasses [to make atonement for us]: and He was raised because we were justified by His death." On this interpretation the significance of the Resurrection for our justification becomes reduced to a "divine declaration that we are accepted with God" (G. B. Stevens, *Pauline Theology*, London, 1892, p. 254; cf. B. Weiss; *Biblical Theology of the New Testament*, Eng. tr., Edinburgh, 1882, i. 437). Its purpose is evidential; it is little more than a certificate or testimonial to the validity of the Death. That the Resurrection has this evidential significance we have seen. But this is only a partial statement of the apostolic view. If this were all, no inner or essential connexion is to be traced between the Resurrection and our justification, but one which is purely external and temporary; and the Resurrection would be a matter which can be dispensed with as soon as faith is gained, or is unnecessary if faith is gained in some other way (see, *e.g.*, Pfleiderer, *Paulinism*, Eng. tr., London, 1877, i. 119).

But this is not adequate to the Pauline thought.

The Resurrection is necessary to our justification, not merely because of the difference it makes to us as certifying the atoning efficacy of the Death and thus evoking faith in us, but also because of the difference it makes to Christ Himself.   It marks the point at which His sovereign power as Lord is made effective.   Our justification, the basis for which has been laid in the Death, becomes an accomplished fact and effective reality only through Christ's rising again, with the virtue of His atoning life and death in Him, to apply His atonement in those who are united with Him by faith.   That which redeems is not Christ's atoning death apart from His living Person into union with whom we are brought by faith.   Nearly every error in theories of the Atonement may be traced ultimately to separating the propitiatory work of Christ from Christ Himself.   The very ABC of Apostolic Christianity is that we are saved not by believing the fact that Christ died for our sins but by union with the Crucified and now Risen Exalted Saviour. Only through union with a living Saviour who has in Him the virtue of His atoning death do justification, forgiveness, and all the blessings of redemption become ours—" In whom we have redemption through his blood " (Eph. i. 7 ; Col. i. 14).   We are accepted " in the beloved " (Eph. i. 6); " there is therefore now no con- demnation to them that are in Christ Jesus " (Rom. viii. 1). Justification is ours as we are " in Christ," in such living union with Him that His life becomes identified with ours and ours with His.   Because of this identification or incorporation Christ's acts are repeated in us so that in His death we die to sin, " crucified with Christ "

(Gal. ii. 20), and in His life we live to righteousness. But it is only by His risen life that Christ can come into such living union with men as thus to effect their redemption.

The apostolic thought accordingly is this : " He was delivered up [to death] on account of our trespasses [to make atonement for them] ; and He was raised on account of our justification [that it might become an accomplished fact]." " His rising again was the necessary antecedent of His applying to His elect the virtue of that Atonement which His dying wrought for all men. . . . He died to purchase what He rose again to apply " (J. H. Newman, *Lectures on the Doctrine of Justification*[3], London, 1874, p. 206). So it is that the resurrection rather than the death of Christ is spoken of as the cause of justification. It is doubtless true, as Denney urges, that " Paul did not make an abstract separation between Christ's Death and His Resurrection, as if the Death and the Resurrection either had different motives, or served ends separable from each other " (*Expos. Gk. Test.*, on Rom. xi. 23–25). Christ's work is one and its end one. He both died and was raised for our justification. But this end was made effective only through the Resurrection ; cf. Rom. viii. 34 : " Who is he that condemneth ? It is Christ that died, yea rather, that was raised from the dead "; v. 10 : " saved by his life "; and 1 Cor. xv. 17 : " If Christ be not risen your faith is futile ; you are still in your sins."

In the Epistle to the Hebrews the same truth is presented from the point of view of the Priesthood of Christ. Just as in Old Testament ritual, only when the high priest took the blood within the veil and sprinkled it upon the Mercy Seat was the offering for sin completed and the covenant-fellowship with God established, so Christ's offering for sin is not completed until in the heavenly sanctuary He presents Himself "through his own blood" (ix. 12), *i.e.* with the virtue of His atoning death in Him. Only then is the new covenant-fellowship between God and sinners established. It is in Him as the living prevailing High Priest, and not merely through something He did in the past, that we have peace with God.

(*b*) Our *sanctification*, our moral and spiritual renewal or quickening, depends upon it. This is but a further explication of (*a*). "In Christ," and through union with Him, we have pardon; "in Christ," and through union with Him, we have sanctification of life. Through His resurrection, therefore, Christ becomes "a life-creating Spirit" (1 Cor. xv. 45), the source of spiritual quickening to believers. Here and now they share in the power of Christ's risen life, whereby they become the subjects of a moral and spiritual resurrection. Through union with Christ by faith, and symbolically in baptism, they are "crucified with Christ" (Gal. ii. 20) unto sin, "engrafted (σύμφυτοι, united vitally) into the likeness of his death" (Rom. vi. 5), the old nature being "annulled" by the introduction through faith into the "in Christ" environment, the environment of the power of the exalted victorious Lord. They rise with Him and live with Him, "engrafted in the likeness of his resurrection," that "like as Christ was raised from the dead through the glory of the Father, so we also might

walk in newness of life" (Rom. vi. 4 ff.; cf. Rom.
viii. 9–11; Eph. ii. 4–7; Col. ii. 12, iii. 1–3; Phil.
iii. 10 f.).

This spiritual resurrection through union with the
Risen Christ St. Paul describes as being "quickened
together with him" and "raised up with him and made
to sit with him in the heavenly places, in Christ Jesus"
(Eph. ii. 4–6). This renewal in which the Christian
life consists is a manifestation in us of "the power of
his resurrection" (Phil. iii. 10), or, as St. Paul more
often puts it, of the same mighty power of God which
had effected Christ's resurrection and enthronement in
the heavenly places, "that working of the strength of
his might which he wrought in Christ, when he raised
him from the dead . . . and (raised) you when ye were
dead through your trespasses and sins" (Eph. i. 19 f.,
ii. 1; cf. 2 Cor. iv. 14). The resurrecting energy of
God in raising Christ and in raising us when we were
dead in trespasses and sins is one and the same. The
one act is the prolongation of the other, the manifestation in two steps or stages of the same Divine miraculous
energy. "Every conversion, every advance in the new
life, is part of that great new creation which began at the
open grave, which advanced at Pentecost, and which will
only reach its consummation when every knee shall bow
to Christ and every tongue confess that He is Lord"
(Cairns, in *Christ and Human Need*, p. 186). St. Paul,
indeed, speaks of the Christian's resurrection and
enthronement as a Divine act "contemporaneous with
the Resurrection and Ascension of Christ" (J. Armitage
Robinson, on Eph. ii. 6), as if it were already achieved.

It is involved in the latter ideally *in posse*, but it has to be worked out really *in esse*.   But one is as much the creative work of His Spirit as the other.   And the outcome of this working of the Spirit St. Paul describes as being "transformed into the same image (εἰκόνα), passing from one glory to another, inasmuch as (this influence proceeds) from the Lord the Spirit" (2 Cor. iii. 18, καθάπερ ἀπὸ Κυρίου πνεύματος).   "Not mere semblance is implied in St. Paul's use of εἰκών, but semblance resting on identity of nature, community of being" (Kennedy, *Last Things*, p. 294).   So that the end is nothing less than perfect assimilation to the very nature of God Himself.

(*c*) The *bodily resurrection* of believers depends upon it.   Already in the Apostolic Age there were those who, under the influence of non-Christian dualistic pre-suppositions, declared that there was nothing more to hope for than a moral and spiritual rising from the dead, that "the resurrection has taken place already" (2 Tim. ii. 18).   And similar attempts are made to-day, under the influence of the dualistic pre-suppositions of modern thought, to confine the resurrection to the moral and spiritual side of our natures, and thus to exclude the physical.   And sometimes the authority of St. Paul is claimed for such a position.   Matthew Arnold, *e.g.*, claims that in St. Paul's teaching the expression "resurrection from the dead" "has no essential con-nexion with physical death. . . . Resurrection, in its essential sense, is . . . for Paul the rising, within the sphere of our visible earthly existence, from death in this sense [obedience to sin] to life in this sense [obedi-

ence to righteousness]. . . . Christ's physical resurrection
after he was crucified is neither in point of time nor
in point of character the resurrection on which Paul,
following his essential line of thought, wanted to fix the
believer's mind. The resurrection Paul was striving
after for himself and others was a resurrection *now*, and
a resurrection to *righteousness* " (*St. Paul and Protestantism*,
ed. London, 1887, p. 55 ff.).

How little this represents St. Paul's point of view may
be seen, not only from the argument in 1 Cor. xv., which
we shall presently consider, but from such a passage as
Rom. viii. 10 ff. where St. Paul impressively reasons
from the indwelling of the Spirit (or the Risen Christ)
in believers, not only to their moral but to their bodily
resurrection. " If Christ is in you, the body is dead
[consigned to physical dissolution] because of sin [of
Adam]; but the spirit [the human spirit of the believer]
is living as the result of righteousness [of Christ]. And,"
he goes on—for the spiritual resurrection which has
already taken place through the indwelling of the Spirit
in the believer is not all—" if the Spirit of him who
raised Jesus from the dead dwells in you, then he who
raised Christ Jesus from the dead will also make your
mortal bodies live by his indwelling Spirit in your lives."
For St. Paul, as for Jewish thought generally, personal
life was an indissoluble unity of soul and body. (On
the Hebrew " synthetic view " of life, see Kennedy, *St.
Paul's Conceptions of the Last Things*, pp. 113, 153, 157.)
There is no trace in his thinking of the Hellenic dualistic
antagonism between body and spirit. And the quickening or " making alive " which is the result of the in-

dwelling πνεῦμα extends to the whole personality'
physical as well as moral and spiritual.

It may be, as Matthew Arnold complains, that
popular theology has confined the idea of the resurrection
both of Christ and of the Christian too much to the
bodily resurrection, thus losing sight of the profoundly
spiritual conception of the Resurrection for apostolic
thought. Jesus had already taught, according to the
Johannine account (John xi. 25 f.; cf. vi. 40, 44, v. 21,
iii. 36), that the root of the resurrection-life lay in living
organic connexion with Him who is the Resurrection and
the Life, and apostolic teaching is in line with this.   The
ground, the operating principle of the resurrection, both
spiritual and physical, of the believer is the indwelling
in him of the life-giving Spirit, the Spirit of the Risen
Christ, or " the Spirit of him that raised up Jesus from
the dead."   The link which makes the Christian
participate in Christ's resurrection is the possession of
His Spirit—" Christ in you the hope of glory" (Col.
i. 27).

Not only is Christ in His resurrection a " firstfruit
(1 Cor. xv. 20, ἀπαρχή) of them that have fallen
asleep," the promise and earnest of the resurrection of
His followers; He is further the ἀρχή (Col. i. 18), the
" first principle " and potency of this resurrection.   As
death was grounded in Adam, so life is grounded in
Christ.   " As in Adam all die [all who belong to Adam's
family], so also in Christ shall all be made alive [all
who belong to Christ] " (1 Cor. xv. 22).   The new life
derived from Christ, that is, includes the body as well as
the soul in the sphere of its quickening.   The indwelling

Spirit is a regenerative principle or power for the whole personality, physical as well as moral, leading not only to a moral resurrection now but to a physical resurrection hereafter. Nay more, this physical quickening whose final fruit and issue is in the resurrection after death, is already begun here on earth, leading to a gradual inward transformation of the body (2 Cor. iv. 16, "renewed from day to day"). Through the indwelling of the Spirit, there is already going on in the believer that subjugation of matter to spirit which in its highest manifestation and outcome was exhibited in the resurrection of Christ's body, transfigured and transformed into a more glorified mode of being, and which, in its final issue in the believer, "shall transform (μετασχηματίσει) the body of our humiliation into conformity with the body of his glory (σύμμορφον τῷ σώματι τῆς δόξης αὐτοῦ), according to the working whereby he is able even to subdue all things to himself" (Phil. iii. 21; cf. 1 John iii. 2).

The moral significance of such a doctrine cannot be overrated. It gives a new sanction to bodily consecration and temperance. Each sin against the body is no longer, as it was on the Greek conception, a stain on that which is itself doomed to perish, but a defilement of that which is consecrated to an eternal life—"Know ye not that your body is a temple of the Holy Ghost?" (1 Cor. vi. 19); "the body is not for fornication, but for the Lord; and the Lord for the body . . . your bodies are members of Christ. . . . Glorify God therefore in your body" (vers. 13–20); "let not sin therefore reign in your mortal body" (Rom. vi. 12); "mortify (do to death) therefore your members which are upon the earth, fornication," etc. (Col. iii. 5).

How different a conception of the future life is this from the current Greek conception familiar to the Corinthians, and prevalent in Jewish-Alexandrian literature. The prospect before St. Paul (and the apostles) is not that of a bodiless state, the deliverance of the soul from its earthly "prison house" ($\sigma\hat{\omega}\mu\alpha$ $\sigma\hat{\eta}\mu\alpha$), but the rising to new life of the entire personality. "We that are in the tabernacle do groan, being burdened,"—St. Paul had just been emphasizing the contrast between the weariness and burden of the present earthly life and the glory which awaits the Christian in the eternal future—"for this reason ($\epsilon\pi\grave{\iota}$ $\tauo\acute{\upsilon}\tau\wp$), not for that we would be unclothed (or stripped, $\epsilon\kappa\delta\acute{\upsilon}\sigma\alpha\sigma\theta\alpha\iota$), but that we would be clothed upon ($\epsilon\pi\epsilon\nu\delta\acute{\upsilon}\sigma\alpha\sigma\theta\alpha\iota$), that what is mortal may be swallowed up of life" (2 Cor. v. 4). These words are sometimes taken as giving expression to an intense desire on St. Paul's part that Christ should come (the Parousia take place) before his death, so that he might be spared the terrifying experience of bodily dissolution, and have the corruptible put on incorruption and the mortal put on immortality without that trial. "If Christ comes first, the Apostle will receive the new body by the transformation, instead of the putting off, of the old; he will, so to speak, put it on *above* the old ($\epsilon\pi\epsilon\nu\delta\acute{\upsilon}\sigma\alpha\sigma\theta\alpha\iota$); he will be spared the shuddering fear of dying; he will not know what it is to have the old tent taken down, and to be left houseless and naked" (Denney, *Expositor's Bible*, "2 Cor.," p. 175 f.; cf. Kennedy, *St. Paul's Conceptions of the Last Things*, p. 266). But it is equally true to the Apostle's thought to interpret the words simply as affirming the Christian conception of the future life as opposed to the Greek conception prevalent in Corinth— this in any case is implied—"We groan, not that we long for a disembodied existence, a condition of spiritual nakedness; rather our longing is for the new embodied condition, the possession of the spiritual body."

Some verses in 2 Cor. v. (especially ver. 8, "We choose rather to be absent from the body and to be present with the Lord") have been held to evidence an advance on St. Paul's part, in the interval between 1 Cor. and 2 Cor., to a more spiritual view of the Resurrection, a disembodied immortality (*e.g.* H. J. Holtzmann, *Lehrbuch der NT Theologie*[2], 2 vols., Tübingen, 1911, ii. 193 ; Charles, *Eschatology*, pp. 397–403). But the words do not justify such a position. St. Paul is simply asserting his confidence that the condition of the

believer which is in prospect (the possession of the σῶμα πνευματικόν), which is guaranteed by the pledge of the πνεῦμα, is in-
finitely preferable to his present condition of being "at home in
the body" (the σῶμα ψυχικόν). And the supposition of a change
of conception on St. Paul's part in his later Epistles—in itself very
unlikely when we consider the short interval between the two
Corinthian Epistles—is decisively negatived by Phil. iii. 21.

The nature of the resurrection-body of believers St.
Paul sets forth in more detail in 1 Cor. xv. 35–42, where
he endeavours to answer the question, "With what kind
of a body (ποίῳ σώματι) do they come?" This was
the difficulty which perplexed the Corinthian Christians,
and led some of them (τίνες, ver. 12) under the influences
of Greek thought to deny altogether the possibility of
a bodily resurrection. Like most similar present-day
objections, the difficulty was based, as St. Paul shows,
upon the supposition that it was the identical body laid
in the grave that was raised again, that the resurrection
meant a revivifying of the present material body, which,
as we have seen, was the current popular Jewish idea,
and which probably formed part of St. Paul's own general
eschatological belief in his pre-Christian Pharisaic days.

By contrast with this false conception of the resurrection St. Paul seeks to elucidate the true nature of the
resurrection-body by means of the analogy or metaphor
of the sowing of seed. It was an analogy already used
by Jesus Himself (John xii. 24), though, as writers of
the " religious-historical " school especially maintain, the
use of this analogy or metaphor from the world of
vegetation may have been suggested to St. Paul by the
prevalence of such nature-myth ideas in popular religious
thought, in which case the analogy would appeal with

peculiar force to his readers (see J. Weiss, on 1 Cor.
xv. 36; cf. Kennedy, *St. Paul's Conceptions of the Last
Things*, p. 241). St. Paul's argument on the basis of
this analogy is directed to remove the objection to the
resurrection of the body derived from its alleged incredi-
bility, and must not be pressed beyond its purpose. It
is as follows:

" What you sow (σὺ ὃ σπείρεις) is not made alive
(ζωοποιεῖται) unless it dies " (ver. 36). The seed
deposited in the earth has to die before it can develop
into a fuller, larger life. The apparent extinction is the
condition of a higher vitality. It is not impossible
therefore, nor even improbable, that our present body
may through death develop into a new and more
perfectly equipped body. The fact that we cannot
beforehand conceive the nature of this body is no valid
objection to the possibility. The same life principle
can clothe itself in altered bodily semblance. Who
could foretell without previous observation what would
spring, *e.g.*, from a grain of wheat? The grain of wheat
itself gives to the eye no token or foreshadowing of the
stalk with ears and grain that is to develop out of it by
God's working in the economy of nature. " What you
sow is not the body that is to be, it is a mere naked
undeveloped grain (γυμνὸν κόκκον) of wheat, *e.g.*, or some
other seed. But God (ὁ δὲ Θεός in contrast to σὺ ὃ
σπείρεις in ver. 36) gives it a body according as He
willed (καθὼς ἠθέλησεν)," rather than as in A. V.
" as He wills "—" the aor. denotes the final act of
God's will determining the constitution of nature "
(T. C. Edwards, *1 Corinthians*², London, 1885, p. 434;

10

cf. Kennedy, *St. Paul's Conceptions of the Last Things*, p. 243; and Charles, *Eschatology, Hebrew, Jewish, and Christian*, p. 392 n.: "We moderns say: The new body is the result of the vital principle in the grain acting on its environment in conformity with God's law in the natural world. St. Paul says in such a case: 'God gives it a body'"). "And to each kind of seed (He gives) a body peculiar to itself (ἴδιον)," the body best fitted to give effective expression to the life which possesses it. The presumption is accordingly that God will find a fit body for man's redeemed nature as He does for each of the seeds vivified in the soil.

"For you must not suppose," St. Paul argues—coming now (ver. 39 f.) to closer quarters with the assumption on which the objection to the resurrection was based, viz. that it is the same identical body that is laid in the grave that is raised up from it—"you must not suppose that there is no other kind of σῶμα than that consisting of σάρξ which you now possess. Even as regards earthly fleshly bodies, there are great varieties in the Divine economy of nature, bodies of men, of beasts, of birds, of fishes, each fitted to life in its own element. And there are not only earthly bodies (σώματα ἐπίγεια) but heavenly bodies (σώματα ἐπουράνια), bodies for heavenly beings just as there are for earthly, and great varieties here also, each fitted to their several distinctive ends or constitution." "So," he says, summing up his discussion on this point, "with the resurrection of the dead, the quickening of the present body through death into another body unimaginably different from it is in the inexhaustible variety of God's resources—for the secret of all is the power of God—as possible and as likely as the springing up of the seed in a wholly different fuller and larger form of life. God, we may well expect, will equip the redeemed life with a body or organism as fitted to the conditions of the future life as the present body is to the conditions of earth."

This future body or organism he describes by contrast with the present body in the following four particulars: " The sowing is in corruption (ἐν φθορᾷ), the rising in incorruption (ἐν ἀφθαρσίᾳ), sown inglorious (ἐν ἀτιμίᾳ) it rises in glory (ἐν δόξῃ), sown in weakness (ἐν ἀσθενείᾳ) it rises in power (ἐν δυνάμει), sown a natural body (σῶμα ψυχικόν) it rises a spiritual body (σῶμα πνευματικόν)" (ver. 43 f.). In the last contrast the root cause or reason of the other contrasts is given. " Corruption," " dishonour," and " weakness " are the characteristics of a " natural " body; " incorruption," " glory," and " power " are the characteristics of a " spiritual " body. " The ψυχή, the natural principle of being, the life-force in the individual, has by God's appointment an organism corresponding to itself, the σῶμα ψυχικόν, the body whose substance is σάρξ, with all which that, in the actual condition of human nature, implies; whose end is necessarily φθορά, decay. . . . The πνεῦμα, on the other hand, the Divine gift, the power which enters human nature in response to faith, and changes it so that henceforward it is governed by a Divine principle, will be equipped with an organism corresponding to itself, the σῶμα πνευματικόν, the ' body ' which has no *fleshly* element inherent in it, which therefore enters upon ἀφθαρσία, incorruption, immortality, as its necessary sphere of existence" (Kennedy, *op. cit.*, p. 252 f.).

Now there is here a difference of interpretation. The first impulse is to refer the "sowing" here spoken of to the burial and dissolution in the grave after death, and the "rising" to the coming forth from the grave after death, the body laid in the grave being the seed out of which the new body is to sprout. (So Bengel, *e.g.* Of σπείρεται he says, "verbum amœnissimum pro sepultura.") But many scholars hold that this is unwarrantably to limit the Apostle's point of view and to confuse his analogy. Our present life, it is held, this life in corruptible flesh, is for St. Paul the sowing time (Gal. vi. 7 ff.), and our mortal bodies (Rom. viii. 10 f.) are in the germinal state, concluding with death, out of which a wholly different organism will spring. The attributes of φθορά (cf. Rom. viii. 21), ἀτιμία (cf. Phil. iii. 21), ἀσθενεία (cf. 2 Cor. xiii. 4) are, it is said, those that St. Paul is wont to ascribe to man's condition in his present state of existence in contrast with the ἀφθαρσία, δόξα, δύναμις of the post-resurrection state (cf. 2 Cor. iv. 7, 10, 16, v. 1, 4; Rom. i. 4, viii. 18–23; see Findlay, *Expos. Gk. Test.*, *in loc.*; Milligan, *Resurrection*, p. 168; Charles, *Eschatology*, p. 392). The difference of interpretation is important for its bearing on the question as to when the process of transformation from the one kind of body to the other takes place, and the latter interpretation is not only truer to the language here used but also more in line with what we have seen to be St. Paul's developed view, that through relation to Christ the resurrection-life,

not only moral but physical, begins here, to be consummated after death (see above, p. 142).

What, however, St. Paul is concerned with in this
passage is primarily the contrast between the two bodies,
the "natural" and the "spiritual," and their genetic
relations. The σῶμα ψυχικόν we have in relation to
Adam, the natural head of the human race, who through
the Divine creative inbreathing became "a living soul"
(ψυχὴ ζῶσα). The σῶμα πνευματικόν we have in
relation to Christ, the second Adam, who through the
Resurrection has become a life-creating Spirit (πνεῦμα
ζωοποιοῦν), the founder and head of a new humanity
(ver. 45). "Man the first is from the earth earthy"
(χοϊκός, "material" [Moffatt]). "Man the second is
from heaven" (ἐξ οὐρανοῦ, ver. 47). (On this contrast
between the "heavenly" man and the "earthly" and its
relation to current Hellenistic ideas, see Weiss, in loc.,
and Feine, Theol. des NT, p. 353.) And "as we have
borne the likeness of the earthly man, so we are to
bear (reading φορέσομεν) the likeness of the heavenly
man" (ver. 49). Not the body of flesh therefore, the
self-expression of the ψυχή, the natural principle of life
which we have in relation to Adam the first member of
the race, is that which will be raised up as the organism
of our future glorious existence, for it is subject to
weakness and corruption. "This I admit, flesh and
blood cannot inherit the kingdom of God, neither doth
corruption inherit incorruption" (ver. 50). This σῶμα
ψυχικόν, the body of our humiliation, shall be exchanged
for a body made like unto (σύμμορφον) the body of
Christ's glory, the body of the Exalted Lord, the second

Adam, who in His risen " heavenly " life possesses a σῶμα πνευματικόν, a body which is the perfect organ and instrument of the Spirit's self-expression. What the substance of this spiritual body is, is not described (is it δόξα ?), only its formative principle. To call it spiritual is not to assert its immateriality or to identify it with spirit, but to affirm its complete subordination to the purposes of spirit. Just as the natural or psychical body does not consist of soul, neither does the spiritual or pneumatical body consist of spirit (cf. Simpson, *Resurrection and Modern Thought*, p. 331).

The support afforded by modern science to the apostolic view of the Resurrection-Body, in particular to St. Paul's doctrine of the "spiritual body" and its connexion with the "natural," is striking and noteworthy. The whole trend of modern psychology is to draw the two sides of man's nature, the bodily and the spiritual, more closely together by emphasizing the dominance of spirit over matter, recognizing that

" . . . of the soule the bodie forme doth take ;
For soule is forme, and doth the bodie make."
(Spenser, *An Hymne in Honour of Beautie*, i. 132 f.)

The identity even of our present bodies is now conceived by science in a less materialistic fashion, as consisting not in identity of the particles of matter of which the body is composed, for this is continually changing, but in that which organizes them and makes them the instrument or medium of its expression, the vital organic constructive principle which in its own nature is spiritual. As Origen expressed it, drawing out the Pauline teaching, " the ' body ' is the same not by any material continuity, but by the permanence of that which gives the law, the 'ratio' (λόγος) . . . of its constitution," the *ratio insita a Deo*, as Jerome translates it (see Westcott, art. "Origenes," *Dict. of Christ. Biog.* iv. 38 n.). Further, the essential meaning of body, science itself is more and more insisting, is the vehicle of manifestation or expression of spirit, and this will take different forms in different conditions of existence. " The real meaning of the bodily life is its spiritual meaning. . . . The bodily being is but vehicle, is but utterance of the spiritual, and the ultimate reality even of the bodily being is only what it is spiritually" (Moberly, *Ministerial Priesthood*, p. 40). "A human body is the necessary—is the only—method and condition, on earth, of spiritual personality. It is capable, indeed, of expressing spirit very badly . . . it is, in fact, almost always falling short of at least the ideal expression of it. And yet body is *the only* method of spiritual life ; even as things are, spirit is the true meaning of bodily life ; and bodies are really vehicles and expressions of spirit ; . . . the perfect ideal would certainly be, not spirit without body, but body which was the ideally perfect utterance of spirit" (Moberly, *Problems and Principles*, p. 358). Admitting the scientific truth of this view of the relation of body and spirit, O. Lodge recognizes the probability of a future embodied state. "Since our identity and personality in no way depend upon identity of material particles, and since our present body has been 'composed' by our characteristic element or soul, it is legitimate to suppose that some other 'body' can equally well be hereafter composed by the same agency ; in other words, that the spirit will retain the power of constructing for itself a suitable vehicle of manifestation, which is the essential meaning of the term 'body'" (*Man and the Universe*, London, 1908, p. 281 f.). In particular, he recognizes the reasonableness of the Christian doctrine of a bodily resurrection. "Christianity both by its doctrines and its ceremonies rightly emphasises the material aspect of existence. For it is founded upon the idea of Incarnation ; and its belief in some sort of bodily resurrection is based on the idea that every real personal existence must have a double aspect—not spiritual alone, nor physical alone, but in some way both. Such an opinion . . . is by no means out of harmony with science. Christianity, therefore, reasonably supplements the mere survival of a discarnate spirit, a homeless wanderer or melancholy ghost, with the warm and comfortable clothing of something that may legitimately be spoken of as a 'body'; that is to say, it postulates a supersensually appreciable vehicle or mode of manifestation, fitted to subserve the needs of future existence as our bodies subserve the needs of terrestrial life" (*Hibbert Journal*, vi. [1907–08] 294 f. ; "The Material Element in Christianity," *ib.* iv. [1905–06] 314 ff., and *Substance of Faith*, London, 1907, p. 106 ; cf. Stewart and Tait's *The Unseen Universe*, London, 1882).

To a great many questions raised by the inquiring mind in this connexion no answer is supplied by the

Apostle. As to the nature of the process or method by which the " natural " body will be changed at the Resurrection into the "spiritual" body, St. Paul never speculates. His interest was practical, not theoretical. He was writing as a missionary, not as a dogmatic theologian, and he confines himself to positive conceptions. It is sufficient for him that he is sure of two things : (1) that the cause or operating principle (ἀρχή) is the power of the new Divine life in the believer's nature, the same power that raised Jesus ; and (2) that the end or consummation of the process is the transformation into the likeness of the body of Christ's glory. In one important respect, indeed, as we have seen (p. 97 ff. above), St. Paul recognizes Christ's resurrection was different from the resurrection of believers. The body of Christ saw no corruption. If Christ's natural body had remained in the grave, no demonstration had been given in His resurrection of that continuity between the earthly body and the risen body which is implied in St. Paul's representation. So St. Paul recognizes two "orders" (1 Cor. xv. 23, τάγματα, groups or divisions) of the risen : the one contains none but Christ the "firstfruit" (ἀπαρχή), who rose on the third day ; the other is composed of those who belong to Christ who shall rise "afterwards" (ἔπειτα), defined as "at the Parousia." But as to *how* they shall rise St. Paul does not speculate.

Again, no information is given as to the Apostle's conception of the state of the believer immediately after death. St. Paul betrays little interest in the question of an Intermediate State, which was so prominent in current

Apocalyptic literature. "The influence upon his heart and mind of the crucified and risen Messiah fixed for ever the point of emphasis in his outlook upon the future. He was able to ignore many aspects of the Last Things on which Jewish and Christian Apocalyptic had set great importance. To go to Christ, to be with Christ, overshadowed all the accompaniments of the End. He knew that nothing could separate His followers from the love of Christ in time or in eternity" (Kennedy, *Last Things*, p. 312). As Wernle succinctly expresses it, the "longing [to be with Christ] spans the chasm that lies between death and the resurrection, and proceeds straight to the desired goal, to the meeting with Jesus" (*Beginnings of Christianity*, i. 287).

So it is that even on a question apparently so important as that of a general resurrection little light is given in St. Paul's writings. His absorbing interest was in the resurrection of believers, the resurrection whose operating principle or $ἀρχή$ is the power of the indwelling Spirit, and the problem of a universal resurrection hardly comes into his view. A resurrection of unbelievers as well as believers is involved in his recognition of a universal judgment at the Final Consummation (Acts xxiv. 15 ; Rom. ii. 5 ff., xiv. 10, 12 ; 1 Cor. vi. 2, xi. 32 ; 2 Cor. v. 10), but such a resurrection occupies a subordinate place in Pauline eschatology and must proceed on different lines. What St. Paul is interested in is the resurrection of Christians, and the other though recognized is not dwelt upon or in any way elaborated—possibly he had not come to definite conclusions on the matter. A resurrection of

the wicked as well as of the righteous was recognized
in Jewish apocalyptic literature (cf. Dan. xii. 2, *Apoc.
Bar.* xxx. 2–5, and 2 Esd. vii. 32–37), though the
more general view in apocalyptic Judaism limited the
scope of the resurrection to the righteous. In the
teaching of Jesus a general resurrection is presupposed.
In John v. 28 f. He speaks of a resurrection of "all
that are in the graves," and distinguishes a "resurrection
of life" (ἀνάστασιν ζωῆς) from a "resurrection of con-
demnation or judgment" (ἀνάστασιν κρίσεως). The
rejection of these verses as an interpolation on the
ground that their teaching is not found in the Synoptics
or elsewhere in John itself is not justified. Charles
(*Eschatology*, p. 371 n.) holds that the doctrine of the
resurrection of the wicked in John is an intrusion due
to Judaistic influence. But a general resurrection of
just and unjust forms at least the background of the
thought in Matt. v. 29 f., x. 28, xii. 41 f., xxv. 31–46 ;
Luke xi. 32 ; John xii. 48.

In the Fourth Gospel, it is true, a profounder view
of the resurrection-life is revealed than that contained
in the Synoptics. The resurrection is represented as
intimately connected with the spiritual renewal or
quickening which comes of organic relationship between
Christ and believers (xi. 25 f. ; cf. vi. 40, 44, v. 21,
iii. 36). So that, while the resurrection in some sense
of unbelievers is affirmed (v. 28 f., xii. 48), it must
have a widely different basis and meaning from that
of believers. It is referred to the omnipotence of the
Father : "the Father raiseth the dead and quickeneth
them" (v. 21). But faith's primary interest is in

" the resurrection of life," the resurrection of those who
are "in Christ," and the apostolic writers often use
language as if there were no other·

So it is that scanty reference is made to a general
resurrection in St. Paul's writings.   Lightfoot (on
Phil. iii. 11) distinguishes firmly between ἡ ἀνάστασις
(or ἐξανάστασις) ἡ ἐκ νεκρῶν and ἡ ἀνάστασις τῶν
νεκρῶν, the former being equivalent to ἀνάστασις ζωῆς,
the latter to ἀνάστασις κρίσεως (John v. 29).   And
some hold that in 1 Cor. xv. 24 there is an explicit
reference to the resurrection of unbelievers, interpreting
τὸ τέλος as " the last act (of the resurrection) " (Meyer)
or " the remainder," the rest of men, those not " in
Christ," as forming a third τάγμα.   According to this
view, a resurrection of believers takes place at the
Parousia, then, after an interval of indefinite duration—
between the point marked by ἔπειτα and the following
εἶτα in which Christ gradually subdues all His enemies
—a resurrection of the wicked (see Lietzmann and
J. Weiss, in loc.).   Such a view finds support in
Rev. xx. 4 f., where, although there is no specific
reference to the resurrection of the wicked, this is
implied in the expression " the first resurrection," as
well as in the connexion established between the
Resurrection and the Judgment.   If any such thought
was in St. Paul's mind here it was at most but a side-
issue in an argument answering the difficulties raised as
to the resurrection of those who have died in Christ.
St. Paul's controlling interest throughout is in the
resurrection of Christians, and for the rest he is content to urge men to the attaining of this resurrection

(Phil iii. 11), and to warn them of the fate attendant on the rejection of Christ (Rom. ii. 5 ; 2 Thess. i. 9 ; cf. 1 Thess. i. 10 ; Phil. iii. 19, etc.).

3. *What it means for the Kingdom of God*

The resurrection of Christ, as thus the ground not only of the moral but of the physical resurrection of believers, is further the pledge and ground of the ultimate dominance of spiritual interests, the consummation of the Kingdom of God. This is its wider cosmic significance.

(*a*) The redemption of the body from the power of death and the grave, St. Paul shows, is an essential part of the Divine world-plan, necessary to the fulfilment of God's Kingdom through Christ (1 Cor. xv. 20–28). Without this Christ is not Lord of all ; " all things " are not subdued unto Him (ver. 27). " Then comes the end (τὸ τέλος, not merely the termination, but the consummation, expressing and manifesting the goal of the whole process) when he shall have abolished every rule (ἀρχήν) and every authority (ἐξουσίαν) and power (δύναμιν) "—every force or power antagonistic to the Divine dominion. " The last enemy to be abolished is death (ὁ θάνατος)." For St. Paul, death, not the mere physical experience, but, as for Hebrew thought generally, this experience in co-relation with sin, was the supreme enemy (see Kennedy, *Last Things*, p. 113). When " he " (ὁ θάνατος—St. Paul almost personifies it ; cf. Heb. ii. 14, " him that had the power of death, that is, the devil," and Rev. xx. 14) has been vanquished,

Christ's dominion is complete. In the resurrection of
Christ we have the assurance that sin and death are
not the final realities in the universe, but are destined
to be swallowed up in victory.

(b) In the redemption of the body through Christ, we
have the pledge of the ultimate subjugation of the entire
material order to the purposes of spirit, the revelation of
the destiny of the whole material universe to be included
in the transformation wrought by Christ. The material
order has shared with the moral and spiritual in the
consequences of sin. It has been "subjected to futility"
(ματαιότητι, Rom. viii. 20), to vain striving; the full
purpose of its existence has been defeated through man's
sin.   Like human life, it is "in thraldom to decay"
(ver. 21, φθορά) and "waits with eager longing" (ver. 19)
for "the freedom of the glory (τῆς δόξης) of the children
of God" (ver. 21). The redemption of the body (ἡ
ἀπολύτρωσις τοῦ σώματος) which is the climax of
material evolution, the rescue of it from the bondage of
φθορά, and the transfiguring and transforming of it so
as to make it the complete instrument of the spirit—
this contains the promise of the transfiguration and
transformation of the entire creation, "new heavens and
a new earth" (2 Pet. iii. 13; Rev. xxi. 1), "all things
new" (Rev. xxi. 5). In the resurrection of Christ as
the pledge and ground of the moral and physical
resurrection of believers we have, accordingly, the assurance that the redemption of Christ involves the rectifi-
cation of the material as well as of the spiritual
universe.   This new condition of things Jesus once
names the "regeneration" or "new birth" (παλινγενεσία,

Matt. xix. 18) of all things.   (St. Peter's phrase in
Acts iii. 21 [ἄχρι χρόνων ἀποκαταστάσεως πάντων]
rendered in A.V. " until the times of restitution of all
things " is hardly a parallel.)

(c) So, finally, in the resurrection of Christ we have
the pledge of the consummation of God's redeeming
purpose—the " summing up (ἀνακεφαλαιώσασθαι) all
things in Christ, the things in heaven, and the things on
earth " (Eph. i. 10), and thus the bringing in of final
world-unity, when " Christ is all and in all " (πάντα καὶ
ἐν πᾶσιν, Col. iii. 11).   For " it pleased (the Father) "—
this was His aim—" through (διά) him to reconcile all
things unto (εἰς) himself . . . whether things upon the
earth, or things in the heavens " (Col. i. 20 ; cf. Phil.
ii. 9–11).   The Resurrection, that is to say, was for the
apostles not only the culmination and completion of the
incarnation and atonement of Jesus ; it was the fulfilment of the original purpose of God in creation, the
consummation or pledge of the consummation of the
whole evolutionary process.   This is expressed most
definitely by St. Paul in Col. i. 15 ff., where Christ, " the
firstborn of all creation " (πρωτότοκος πάσης κτίσεως),
its norm and type, that which sets for it its true end—
" for in him were all things created, in the heavens and
upon the earth . . . all things have been created through
him, and unto [with a view to] him " (εἰς αὐτόν, ver.
15 ff.)—is described as the beginning (ἀρχή, the first
principle), the first begotten from the dead in order that
He might become (ἵνα γένηται) pre-eminent over all (ἐν
πᾶσιν, " no doubt purposely left indefinite, including
every province of creation " [Kennedy, *St. Paul's Concep-*

tions of the Last Things, p. 298]).   Through the Resurrection, as the culmination of the Incarnation and Atonement, by means of which Christ becomes the ἀρχή or life-giving principle of a new humanity, God's aim in the whole process of creation attains its end.

LITERATURE. — On the significance of the Resurrection see **W. Milligan**, *Resurrection of our Lord*, London, 1881, lects. iv., v., vi. ; **B. F. Westcott**, *Gospel of the Resurrection*[7], do., 1891, chs. ii. and iii. ; **S. D. F. Salmond**, *Christian Doctrine of Immortality*[4], Edinburgh, 1901, bks. iv., v., vi. ; **J. Orr**, *Resurrection of Jesus*, London, 1908, ch. x. ; **D. W. Forrest**, *Christ of History and of Experience*[7], Edinburgh, 1914, lect. iv. ; **E. Griffith-Jones**, *The Ascent through Christ*[6], London, 1901, bk. iii. chs. i. and ii. ; **W. J. Sparrow Simpson**, *Resurrection and Modern Thought*, do., 1911, bk. iii., art. "Resurrection of Christ," in *DCG* ii. 512 ; **B. Lucas**, *The Fifth Gospel*, London, 1907, p. 160 ff. ; **D. S. Cairns**, "The Risen Christ," in *Christ and Human Need*, do., 1912, p. 176 f. ; **H. Scott Holland**, "The Power of the Resurrection," in *Miracles*, do., 1911, p. 118 ff. ; **S. Eck**, "Die Bedeutung der Auferstehung Jesu für die Urgemeinde und für uns," in *Hefte zur christlichen Welt*, xxxii. [1898] ; **R. H. Grützmacher**, *Modern-positive Vorträge*, Leipzig, 1906, pp. 109–129, "Jesu Auferstehung und der Mensch der Gegenwart."

CHAPTER IX

ATTEMPTED NATURALISTIC OR SEMI-NATURAL-ISTIC EXPLANATIONS OF THE APOSTOLIC BELIEF

THE character and significance of the apostolic belief in the resurrection of Christ have now been considered, and the historical evidence on which the belief was based. It remains to review the attempts which have been made to account for the apostolic belief and its consequences without acknowledging the full fact of the Resurrection, as this is represented in the apostolic writings.

I. OLDER FORMS OF EXPLANATION

Some of the older naturalistic hypotheses may now be regarded as obsolete and abandoned. They have practically only a historical or antiquarian interest, and do not need to be re-argued at length. Yet they are not on that account to be overlooked. As monuments not only recording past history, but serving as warnings to all time of the futility of certain methods of explanation, they demand passing notice.

1. *The Swoon Theory*

According to this theory, Jesus' supposed death on the Cross was in reality only a swoon, a case of "suspended animation." In the cool air of the cavern tomb He revived and again appeared among His disciples. This explanation — a favourite one in the school of eighteenth century rationalism, and associated especially with the name of Paulus—is now hopelessly discredited. To escape with His life after having been nailed to the Cross meant that the Resurrection, if resurrection it could be called, was a return to life under the same conditions as before, and this, as we have seen, is not the kind of fact with which the records deal. The practical difficulties of the theory are insuperable. If Jesus had presented Himself merely as one who had stolen half-dead out of the sepulchre, His appearance would have produced the impression of weakness and helplessness, not that of a conqueror over death and the grave. (For a trenchant statement of these practical difficulties see Strauss, *New Life of Jesus*, i. 412.)

2. *The Theft or Fraud Theory*

A second hypothesis, which may also be taken as now practically discredited, is the theory that the disciples, in order that they might still have a message, stole the body and pretended that Jesus had risen. The theory is an old one—the oldest of all indeed, if we may believe the story of Matt. xxv. 11–15, which was still current in the days of Justin Martyr (*Dial. with Trypho*, 17). The theory thus anticipated by the Jewish authorities was urged, though with some difference of detail, by Celsus (see Origen, *c. Cels.* ii. 56). It is identified in modern times chiefly with the name of Reimarus. The theory thus stated would found Christianity on imposture or fraud. But no sober critic now challenges the good faith of the first disciples in their witness. They "really had the impression of having seen him" (Schmiedel, *Encycl. Bibl.* iv. 4061). A more recent form of the theory is that adopted by O. Holtzmann (*Life of Jesus*, p. 499), that the body was quietly removed by the owner of the grave without the knowledge of the disciples. Joseph of Arimathæa, feeling, on reflexion, that it would not do to have in his respectable family vault the body of a man who had been crucified, had the body of Jesus secretly removed and buried elsewhere. Another form of the theory is that suggested by A. Réville (see *Jésus de Nazareth. Études critiques sur les antécédents de l'histoire évangélique*, Paris, 1897, ii. 420 ff.), that the leaders of the Sanhedrin bribed the soldiers to remove the body lest the tomb might become an object of pilgrimage to Jesus' followers in Galilee, and fanatical outbreaks might occur in Jerusalem. Lake gives what he holds to be a more possible hypothesis. His suggestion is that the women in the dusk of the morning came to a tomb which they thought was the one in which they had seen the Lord buried. "They expected to find a closed tomb, but they found an open one; and a young man, who was in the entrance, guessing their errand, tried to tell them that they had made a mistake in the place. 'He is not here,' said he; 'see the place where they laid him,' and probably pointed to the next tomb. But the women were frightened at the detection of their errand and fled, only imperfectly or not at all understanding what they heard" (*The*

Resurrection of Jesus Christ, p. 251 f.).   B. H. Streeter (in *Foundations*, London, 1912, p. 134) claims that "with a little ingenuity it is not difficult to imagine more than one set of circumstances which might account on purely natural grounds for the tomb being found empty."

But, apart altogether from the consideration that the theory in these different forms contradicts the historical evidence in vital points, and that to ascribe to fraud or mistake the rise of a belief with such revolutionary effects in the thought and life of the disciples is altogether improbable as an adequate explanation, there is one fact on which all such theories come to grief.   Within a few weeks of the Death and the Burial (fifty days after, on the day of Pentecost) the disciples were boldly proclaiming in the streets of the very city where Jesus had been crucified, and even before the authorities who were responsible for the Crucifixion, that God raised Him up on the third day, and through this public proclamation were making multitudes of converts.   If their testimony was false, why did not the Jewish and Roman authorities for ever silence the disciples by pointing to where the body of Jesus still lay, or by showing how it had come to be removed from the tomb in which it had been laid after the Crucifixion ?   What could have been at once easier and more effective ?   Even after an interval of fifty days, as medical science acknowledges, the body must have been recognizable.   " The silence of the Jews is as significant as the speech of the Christians " (Fairbairn, *Studies in the Life of Christ*, p. 357).   " *Did not* in this case spells *could not*, and the empty tomb remains an unimpeachable witness to the truth of the message that the Lord had risen " (Orr, *Resurrection of Jesus*, p. 213 f.).

3. *The Subjective Vision or Mental Hallucination Theory*

This is the most weighty of the older theories put forward to explain the apostolic belief in the Resurrection, without acknowledging the actual fact.   According to this theory the so-called "appearances" of the Risen Christ were due to the excited state of mind in which the disciples were after the death of their Master. Overwrought and mentally distraught by the shock of His death, and yearning for His presence, they saw apparitions or visions of Him.   But these were purely subjective—phantasms or mental hallucinations.   They longed to see Him; they expected to see Him; and they thought they did see Him.   Their thought was perfectly honest, but it was nevertheless a hallucination. For persons in a state of unusual mental excitement and expectancy, especially when they are also of a highly strung nervous temperament, such visions are, it is represented, common phenomena of religious history, and are often contagious.   So it was in the case of the appearances of Jesus.   They began with the women, probably with Mary Magdalene, an excitable and nervous person.   Her story that she had seen the Lord was eagerly embraced; it spread with lightning rapidity, and with the force of an epidemic.   What she believed she had seen others believed they too must see, and they saw. The visions were the product of their dwelling in fond and affectionate memory on the personality of their Master, which, after the first shock of despair was over, they came to feel was such that He must have survived death. So it is that Renan represents the case. As he puts it, " Ce qui a ressuscité Jésus, c'est l'amour " (*Les Apôtres*, Paris, 1866, ch. i., Eng. tr., London, 1869). With this Strauss combines reflexion upon certain passages of the Old Testament expressing faith in the Resurrection, together with recollection of the Master's own predictions of the fact.

The inadequacy of such a theory to account for a belief with such incalculably momentous results as the belief in the Resurrection has often been exposed, but because of its continued prevalence in one form or other in the present day—such recent critics as Schmiedel, Weizsäcker, Harnack, A. Meyer, and Loisy support it— the chief objections to it, in addition to the fundamental consideration referred to in last section (see p. 164), which applies equally against all forms of the vision theory, may be briefly indicated.

(1) Such a psychological condition as is necessary to the vision theory is absent on the disciples' part. With hearts sad and hopes broken, so far from expecting a Resurrection, they could hardly be persuaded of the fact even after it occurred (Luke xxiv. 11 ; John xx. 9–25 ; Mark xvi. 11, 13). The women themselves who went on the third morning to the tomb went to anoint a dead body, not to behold a Risen Lord. (2) With reference to Strauss's attempt to base the expectation on certain passages of the Old Testament, there is no evidence of

any Jewish belief in Jesus' time of a resurrection from the dead before the last day, much less of such a resurrection as took place in the case of Jesus (see Edersheim, *Life and Times*[4], ii. 624). Even Jesus' own intimations that He would rise again, frequently as they were given (*e.g.* Matt. xvi. 21, xvii. 9, xx. 19, xxvi. 32, etc., and parallels), seem to have made no impression upon the disciples. The thought was so strange to them that they were unable to receive it. Only after the event were these predictions understood (cf. John ii. 22). (3) The tradition of " the third day " and of the appearances already on this day of the Risen Christ in Jerusalem is set aside as affording too little time for the rise of visions. So the upholders of the vision theory feel the necessity of transferring the appearances of Jesus from Jerusalem to Galilee, thus not only giving more time for visions to develop, but transferring them to scenes where memory and imagination could more easily work. This involves the separating them from the empty tomb and the events of the Easter morn, which we have seen to be facts firmly rooted in the apostolic tradition. The inadequacy of Strauss's endeavour to show how the belief in " the third day " may have originated from Old Testament hints (*New Life*, i. 438 f.) has already been referred to above, p. 57 f. (4) The fact that the manifestations were made not merely to this or that individual but to companies of persons at the same time, " the twelve," " all the apostles," " more than five hundred," increases many-fold the difficulty of explaining as the product of subjective vision the fact to which they bear witness. There are no doubt genuine instances of

" collective " delusion, an impression received or idea
conceived by one ardent soul being transmitted by a
kind of electric sympathy to others ready to bear witness
that they have had a like experience.   Schmiedel gives
some instances (*Encycl. Bibl.* iv. 4083) ; but there is
this fundamental difference between these and the
appearings of the Risen Christ, that in the latter case,
as the narratives bear distinctly on their face, the whole
company was instantaneously affected in the same way.
(5) The theory is inconsistent with the fact that the
visions came so suddenly to an end.   After the forty
days no appearing of the Risen Lord is recorded, except
that to St. Paul, the circumstances and object of which
were altogether exceptional.   It is not thus that imagina-
tion works.   As Keim says, " the spirits that men call
up are not so quickly laid " (*Jesus of Nazara*, vi. 357).

4. *The Objective Vision or Telegram Hypothesis*

Keim, realizing the difficulties of the last theory,
advanced the hypothesis that the appearances, while
essentially of the nature of visions, were not purely subjective—the result of the enthusiasm and mental excitement of the disciples—but real, objectively caused
manifestations of the Risen Christ.   His theory is that,
while the body of the Crucified Jesus remained in the
tomb, His living spirit sent telegrams to the disciples to
assure them that He still lived, telegrams or supernatural manifestations which the disciples took for *bona
fide* bodily appearances of their Risen Master (*Jesus of*

Nazara, vi. 364). Keim thinks that in this way he saves the truth of the Resurrection. " Though much has fallen away, the secure faith-fortress of the resurrection of Jesus remains " (p. 365).

A more recent presentation of the same type of theory is given by Streeter in *Foundations,* p. 127 ff. The appearances, while they may be styled " visions," are yet not subjective but " directly caused by the Lord Himself veritably alive and personally in communion with them " (p. 136). Our Lord as Spirit acting in the spiritual sphere he represents as " able to convince His disciples of His victory over death by some adequate manifestation ; possibly by showing Himself to them in some form such as might be covered by St. Paul's phrase ' a spiritual body ' ; possibly through some psychological channel similar to that which explains the mysterious means of communication between persons commonly known as telepathy ; or possibly in some way of which at present we have no conception " (p. 136).

The aim of the theory is, while acknowledging a kind of resurrection, to relieve the mind from the difficulty of believing in an actual resurrection of the body from the grave. The root of the theory is thus aversion to the recognition of the supernatural in the physical realm. In such a theory, Keim himself acknowledges, the supernatural is not altogether eliminated. " Christian faith . . . oversteps these boundaries [of the natural order], not merely in the certain assurance that Jesus . . . took his course to the higher world of God and of spirits . . . but also in the conviction that it was he and no other who, as dead yet risen again, as celestially glorified even if not risen, vouchsafed visions to his disciples" (p. 360). The intervention of the supernatural in the normal mental, or psychological order of the disciples' experience is thus presumed.   Once we admit such an intervention, however, there is no reason why we should not proceed further to the full apostolic affirmation—for which this is a poor substitute—that Jesus burst the bands of death and came forth bodily from the tomb on the morning of the third day.

Of this theory Bruce remarks that it is "a bastard supernaturalism as objectionable to unbelievers as the true supernaturalism of the Catholic creed, and having the additional drawback that it offers to faith asking for bread a stone" (*Apologetics*, p. 393).   Besides, there is the further difficulty urged by Bruce that Keim's hypothesis requires us to believe that the faith of the Christian Church is based upon a revelation from heaven which was in fact misleading.   " Christ sends a series of telegrams from heaven to let His disciples know that all is well.   But what does the telegram say in every case?   Not merely, My Spirit lives with God and cares for you ; but, My body is risen from the grave. . . . If the resurrection be an unreality, if the body that was nailed to the tree never came forth from the tomb, why send messages that were certain to produce an opposite impression ? " (*ib.*).   The hypothesis really means that Christ deceives His disciples by inducing them, and through them the whole Christian Church, to believe a lie.   The new turn given to the theory by psychical research will be considered below (p. 175 ff.).

LITERATURE.—For criticism of older theories see **T. Keim**, *Jesus of Nazara*, Eng. tr., 6 vols., London, 1873–83, vi. ; **A. B. Bruce**, *Apologetics*, Edinburgh, 1892, pp. 383–398 ; **W. Milligan**, *Resurrection of our Lord*, London, 1881, lect. iii. ; **J. Orr**, *Resurrection of Jesus*, do., 1908, ch. viii. ; **A. M. Fairbairn**, *Studies in the Life of Christ*, do., 1881, ch. xviii. ; **Macpherson**, *The Resurrection of Jesus Christ*, Edinburgh and London, 1867.

CHAPTER X

ATTEMPTED NATURALISTIC OR SEMI-NATURAL-ISTIC EXPLANATIONS OF THE APOSTOLIC BELIEF (*Continued*)

II. MORE RECENT EXPLANATIONS

THE character of the attack on the Resurrection in recent times has changed in some important respects. New knowledge and new critical methods have given rise to new ways of attempting to explain the belief in the Resurrection without accepting the full facts presented in the apostolic narratives. A close relation exists between these different theories—they are but different aspects of the same attempt to remove or minimize the supernatural in Christianity — but different forms can be distinguished according to the difference of emphasis.

1. *The Psychological or Psychical Research Theory*

A new turn, and with it a new vogue, has been given to the objective vision theory in recent times by bringing the appearings of the Risen Christ recorded in the narratives into line with the phenomena of psychical

research. The late F. W. H. Myers, one of the leaders
in this movement, held that psychical research had
definitely established the reality of telepathic intercommunication between this world and another.
" Observation, experiment, inference, have led many
inquirers, of whom I am one, to a belief in direct or
telepathic intercommunication, not only between the
minds of men still on earth, but between minds or spirits
still on earth and spirits departed" (*Human Personality
and its Survival of Bodily Death*, p. 350). And so
highly did Myers estimate the worth of the evidence
supplied by these psychical investigations that he
predicted that "in consequence of the new evidence, all
reasonable men, a century hence, will believe the
Resurrection of Christ, whereas, in default of the new
evidence, no reasonable men, a century hence, would
have believed it" (*ib.* p. 351). The ground of this
prediction he proceeds to state : "Our ever-growing
recognition of the continuity, the uniformity of cosmic
law has gradually made of the alleged *uniqueness* of
any incident its almost inevitable refutation . . . and
especially as to that central claim, of the soul's life
manifested after the body's death, it is plain that this
can less and less be supported by remote tradition alone ;
that it must more and more be tested by modern
experience and inquiry " (*ib.*).

The position thus stated has found considerable
support, among both theologians and scientists. It is to
" the type of phenomena collected by the Society of
Psychical Research, and especially by the late Mr. F. W.
H. Myers," that Lake, *e.g.*, turns for help in understand-

ing the nature of the appearances of the Risen Christ (*The Resurrection of Jesus Christ*, p. 272). As to the results already obtained in this sphere he expresses himself more cautiously than Myers. He thinks it possible that at least " some evidence " already exists pointing to the fact of such communications having taken place. But "we must wait until the experts have sufficiently sifted the arguments for alternative explanations of the phenomena, before they can actually be used as reliable evidence for the survival of personality after death" (p. 245). As to the value of the evidence, however, when thus sifted and substantiated, Lake has no doubt. The belief in the Resurrection even in the sense of the personal survival of Jesus after death depends on the success of the experiments and investigations of psychical research. It must remain "merely an hypothesis until it can be shown " through these experiments and investigations " that personal life does endure beyond death, is neither extinguished nor suspended, and is capable of manifesting its existence to us " (*ib.*). Some of the leading representatives of present-day science, too, have found in the phenomena of psychical research new support in favour of belief in the recorded appearances of Christ after His death. Sir Oliver Lodge, *e.g.*, maintains that the narratives of the appearances are substantially accurate records of genuine psychical experiences on the part of the apostles. The appearances during the forty days are mysterious enough, but they can be accepted very much as they stand, for they agree with our experience of genuine psychical phenomena the world over (cf. *Man and the Universe*, p. 290). And more recently Sir Conan Doyle has declared himself a convert to the theory (see specially *The New Revelation*, London, 1918). This relating of the appearances of the Risen Christ to psychical phenomena is held to explain some of the difficulties belonging to the narratives, in particular the apparent discrepancy in regard to the locality of the appearances (see *Resurrectio Christi*, London, 1909; *Interpreter*, vi. [1909-10] 306).

Now this branch of psychological science is still in its infancy, and it is difficult to speak yet of any definiteness of results. But already it is evident that a new chapter in the discussion of the Resurrection has opened here. The whole question of the relation of body and spirit has taken on a new aspect through these investigations. The mystery of human personality and the possession of hitherto unrecognized powers, not only of mind over mind, but of mind over body, is being revealed as never before. The evidences of hypernormal mental control, especially in the hypnotic state, over bodily processes (*e.g.* the production of blisters and ecchymoses of the skin, the so-called " stigmata " by verbal suggestion) show that mind has the power of exerting a far greater influence over body than had been generally recognized by psychologists (see, *e.g.*, MacDougall, *Body and Mind*, ch. xxv.). And the evidence produced by such investigations of the control of matter by spirit in extraordinary if not preternatural ways may aid not a little in removing prejudice to the facts recorded in the narratives as to the resurrection and ascension of Christ. " When scientists of worldwide reputation, trained in the strictest school of scientific inquiry, such as Sir William Crookes, Sir Oliver Lodge, and Sir Alfred Wallace, declare, as they have done, that they have verified the fact by repeated experiment that ponderable bodies can be moved without physical contact by some hitherto unrecognized force which was brought into play by the action of human will, it is no longer possible to treat with scientific contempt the assertions contained in the Gospels that Christ's material body disappeared from the tomb as the result of a hitherto unrecognized force which was exerted upon it without physical contact" (Robinson, *Studies in the Resurrection*, p. 97). This indeed seems to be so far the chief value or function of these investigations—what may be called a preparatory or prolegomenary function. For minds approaching the subject of the future life and personal survival after death from the scientific point of view and under the influence of materialistic or semi-materialistic assumptions, they have been able to remove objections based on these assumptions and thus cleared the way for a more positive belief on the subject, making it at least credible. So it has been, *e.g.*, in the case of Conan Doyle (see his own confession in *The New Revelation*, p. 17 ff.). And in the interests of truth fuller investigation of the facts by scientific experts— experimental psychologists and leaders of the medical profession—is demanded. It is doubtful, however, how far help can be obtained from this quarter in understanding the kind of Resurrection recorded in the narratives and in supporting the belief in the future which is based on the new revelation contained therein.

12

The attitude of most critics will, we fancy, at present be one of non-committal or suspended judgment.

Against the attempt to bring the resurrection of Christ into line with the phenomena dealt with by psychical research and to make belief in the Resurrection dependent on the scientific verification of these pheno- mena in the way that Myers and Lake suggest, the following objections may be urged :

(1) It does less than justice to the apostolic claim. According to Myers the "essential claim" of the tradition of Christ's resurrection is taken to be "the soul's life manifested after the body's death." Its claim extends, that is to say, only to a spiritual Resurrection, a Resurrection in the sense of a personal survival of Jesus, an assurance that though His body was laid in the tomb and remained there He lived in spirit. "What we mean by resurrection is not resuscitation of the material body, but the unbroken survival of personal life" (Lake, p. 265). So it is held that "the existence of verified apparitions would substantiate all that is useful in the study of the resurrection, and make human experience in all ages akin" (J. H. Hyslop, *Psychical Research and the Resurrection*, Boston, 1908, p. 383). As for a physical resurrection, "this must remain incredible so long as such phenomena are not now frequent, and as long as human experience does not reproduce it as a law of nature" (*ib.*). But it was not upon such spiritual apparitions or "manifestations of a surviving personality" that the faith of the Church in the resurrection of Christ was built; it was, as we have seen, upon His victory over death and the grave, as

witnessed by the empty tomb on the third day and His subsequent appearings.

(2) To place the appearings of the Risen Christ on the same level as spiritualistic apparitions of the dead—no more miraculous or significant than they—given to assure the sorrowing disciples that their Master was still living in the world of spirits, thus "making human experience in all ages akin," is to eliminate just that which is of distinctive worth and value in His appearings, and to fail to realize the true significance of the Resurrection for apostolic thought. The Resurrection claims to be a new beginning, a new departure in experience, not the exhibition of a mere "survival" or continued existence after death, but the revelation of a new mode or order of life, and as such a revelation *sui generis*. For the apostles the Resurrection had a significance far beyond the incidental revelation of the truth that Christ lives on after death. It was a fact of the largest moral and spiritual significance, for it meant His exaltation at the right hand of God, supreme in the material as well as in the spiritual world, and as such led to a revolution in apostolic thought and life. To compare the appearings and manifestations of the Risen Christ, with their unique and far-reaching results, to the spiritualistic apparitions of psychical research and alleged communications from the other world is to compare the incomparable. When any of the " resurrections " investigated by the Society for Psychical Research has consequences of a moral and spiritual character to be compared with the New Testament or the Apostolic Church—then, but not till then, will we believe it is the

same kind of thing as the resurrection of Jesus. So-called "messages" or "communications" from the other side of death we have in abundance, but for the most part they are mere inanities and platitudes which we are as well without. "If communication is established at all with the spirit-world, it is merely with 'the dregs and lees of the unseen universe'—with spirits who either have not the power or else the will to communicate anything of importance to man" (W. P. Paterson, in Hastings' Smaller *Dict. of Bible*, p. 458ᵃ).

(3) The reality of the alleged communications from the unseen is at least open to question. It is always conceivable that they are due to as yet little understood supernormal or abnormal powers of the human personality, such as subconscious suggestion assisted by telepathy or thought-transference between those conducting the inquiry. In any case, a scientific proof or verification of the Resurrection by experimental methods on evidence open to all alike, such as Myers and Lake desiderate, would have no religious value. The belief in the resurrection of Jesus depends on an initial appreciation of the uniqueness of His personality, on a moral and spiritual evaluation—it is belief in *Jesus* as risen, and this is spiritually conditioned. The attempt to attain belief in the fact by experimental means is not only sub-Christian, it is sub-spiritual—it is naturalism in religion (cf. R. C. Moberly, *Atonement and Personality*, London, 1907, p. 310, "Spiritualism is the nemesis of unspirituality").

(4) The object of the theory is to bring the resurrection of Christ into line with natural phenomena and "our

ever-growing recognition of the continuity, the uniformity
of cosmic law" (Myers, *Human Personality*, p. 351),
and thus to get rid of the supernatural especially in the
physical realm.   The empty tomb and the event on the
third day become, on this theory, mistakes for which
some explanation has to be found.   What Lake's
suggested explanation is has already been considered
(see above, p. 163).

LITERATURE.—On this theory see **F. W. H. Myers**, *Human Person-
ality and its Survival of Bodily Death*, ed. London, 1907 ; **K. Lake**,
Historical Evidence for the Resurrection of Jesus Christ, do., 1907 ;
O. Lodge, *Survival of Man*, do., 1909, art. "The Immortality of the Soul,"
pt. ii., in *Hibbert*, vi. [1908] 574 ff., *Raymond* ; **F. Podmore**, *The Newer
Spiritualism*, London, 1910 ; **W. F. Barrett**, *On the Threshold of the
Unseen*[2], do., 1917 ; **J. H. Hyslop**, *Psychical Research and the
Resurrection*, Boston, 1908 ; **Gerald Balfour** in *Proceedings of the
Aristotelian Society*, "The Ear of Dionysius" ; **A. E. Taylor**, in *Faith
and the War*, London, 1916, 130 ff. ; **C. H. Robinson**, *Studies in
the Resurrection of Christ*, do., 1909, ch. viii. ; **W. MacDougall**, *Body
and Mind*, do., 1911, ch. xxv. ; **B. H. Streeter**, and others, *Immortality*,
do., 1917, Essays ii. and vii. ; **Edward Clodd**, *The Question* : A brief
History and Examination of Modern Spiritualism, do., 1917 ; **Jane T.
Stoddart**, *The Case against Spiritualism*, do., 1919.

2. *The Mythological Theory*

A second characteristic modern form of explanation
of the Apostolic belief in the Resurrection is the theory
adduced from the side of the study of comparative
religion and mythology is perhaps the most characteristic modern form of explanation.   It is connected, in
its most recent phase, with the rise of the school of
thought usually called " Neo-Babylonian " or " Pan-Baby-
lonian " from its attempt to account for much in Bible
story through the influence of conceptions imported into

Judaism from the Orient, and derived chiefly from Babylonia.

The fundamental principle of this school or movement in relation to Christianity is the demand that the religion of Jesus Christ, including its Old Testament preparation, be studied by the scientific - historical method, not as if it were something unique and apart, "a holy island in the sea of history," but in its place in the stream, and in essential connexion with religions chronologically and geographically adjacent to it. As applied to the New Testament, the attitude of the school may be represented by the thesis of H. Gunkel that "in its origin and shaping (*Ausbildung*) in important and even in some essential points the religion of the New Testament stood under the influence of foreign religions, and that this influence was transmitted to the men of the New Testament through Judaism" (*Zum religions-geschichtlich. Verständnis des NT*, Göttingen, 1903, p. 1); or by that of Cheyne: "There are parts of the New Testament—in the Gospels, in the Epistles, and in the Apocalypse—which can only be accounted for by the newly-discovered fact of an Oriental syncretism, which began early and continued late (*Bible Problems*, p. 19). Among the beliefs thus accounted for is the belief in the resurrection of Jesus in the form in which this appears in the New Testament. Myths of the death and resurrection of gods, "resurrection legends," derived ultimately from Babylonia, were spread, it is represented, through the whole East, and these, entering through many channels, chiefly through the mystery-religions, became attached first to the figure of the expected Messiah in Jewish literature, and then through Judaism to Jesus of Nazareth, and had a powerful influence in moulding the New Testament representation of His resurrection.

It is nothing new to draw comparisons or analogies between the New Testament story of the resurrection of Jesus and the myths of the death and resurrection of gods in pagan religions. Celsus had already made a beginning in this direction. He compared the New Testament narratives of the Resurrection with similar myths in Greek story (see Origen, *c. Cels.* ii. 55 f.). What is characteristic of this new scientific school of thought is that it is no longer comparisons or analogies merely which are sought between the Gospel narratives and pagan myths, but an actual derivation the one from the other. Gunkel, *e.g.*, thus derives from Oriental, and ultimately from Babylonian, conceptions, the New Testament story of the Resurrection from the dead on the third day (*op. cit.* pp. 76–83; cf. pp. 31–35), the Ascension (*ib.* p. 71 f.), and the origin of Sunday as a Christian festival (*ib.* pp. 73–76). And Cheyne holds that "the apostle Paul, when he says (1 Cor. xv. 3 f.) that Christ died and that He rose again 'according to the Scriptures,' in reality points to a pre-Christian sketch of the life of Christ, partly . . . derived from widely - spread non - Jewish myths, and embodied in Jewish writings" (*Bible Problems*, p. 113). This is the theory of Strauss over again, with the substitution of Babylonian mythology for Old Testament prophecy.

In criticism of such an attempted derivation of the apostolic belief in the Resurrection it has to be said:

(1) That the fundamental assumption or allegation on which the application of the theory to the New Testament story depends, viz. the influence of Oriental conceptions on Jewish thought in the way of giving rise to a pre-Christian sketch of a dying and rising Messiah, is unjustified. That Jewish thought in the time of Christ was familiar with the idea of a resurrection of the dead —a resurrection of the body at the last day—is certain (though Gunkel's attempt to trace its origin to extra-Jewish Oriental sources must be contested; see Kennedy, *St. Paul's Conceptions of the Last Things*, p. 64). But that the idea of a dying and rising Messiah formed part of this thought, that the idea of a resurrection from the dead was connected with the Messiah in current Jewish beliefs, is contrary to evidence. The notion of a resurrection of the Messiah had nothing corresponding to it in the beliefs of Judaism. Even when Jesus had given repeated intimations of His death and resurrection, and had represented this as in accordance with Old Testament prophecy, so contrary was the idea to contemporary Judaism that the disciples themselves were "slow of heart" to believe the things that Jesus had spoken to them (Luke xxiv. 25 f., 44–46).

(2) Not only is the fundamental assumption of the theory without support, but the analogies quoted between the New Testament and extra-Jewish mythological thought are altogether inadequate for the purpose in view. If God is in all history we may expect to find a preparation for the higher in the lower, in the way of foreshadowings or prefigurations of Christian truths in ethnic religions. But the analogies cited to explain the

Christian ideas are no real parallels. Take, *e.g.*, the mythological explanations of the Resurrection on the third day. Why was the third day fixed upon for the occurrence? Strauss maintained that it was because of Old Testament hints. The insufficiency of such an answer Gunkel and Cheyne acknowledge, and they claim that the matter can be satisfactorily explained only from the religious-historical point of view, as due to the influence of pagan myths of solar deities on Jewish thought. "The three days" of Jonah and "the three and one half" of Dan. (vii. 25, xii. 7) and the Apocalypse (xi. 12, 14) are all forms of Oriental sun-god myths (Gunkel, p. 82 ff.; Cheyne, p. 110 ff.). To this influence also is due the observance of Sunday as the day of the commemoration of the Resurrection. The Lord's Day was the day of the sun-god. Easter Sunday was the day of the sun's emergence from the night of winter (Gunkel, pp. 74, 79). It is not strange that this was the day on which Jesus was said by the primitive Christian community to have risen. It is really an ancient Oriental festival which has here been taken over by the early Church. But a borrowed story ought at least to have some real likeness to its source, and there is no true analogy between the story of Christ's death and resurrection on the third day and the pagan myths of slain and risen gods, beyond the general ideas of death and survival. These myths were polytheistic in origin, and were a poetic rendering of the phenomena of the yearly death and revival of vegetation represented in ritual and personified. The death and resurrection of Christ, on the other hand, were historical facts which bore no relation whatever to these myths. The resurrection of Attis, Adonis, and Osiris was an annual affair symbolizing the sun's victory over winter in spring. The resurrection of Christ, however, was commemorated not only once a year at Easter, but also every Sunday. Had it been suggested by pagan myths and rituals, its commemoration would have shown some trace at least of the rites which suggested the belief, but nothing such is found. That Christ's death and resurrection took place at the time of such a pagan commemoration may be regarded as a coincidence and nothing more, although it may have had some influence in furthering the acceptance of the story itself among pagans. The pagan beliefs in slain and risen gods, therefore, bear no real likeness to the account of Christ's death and resurrection in the New Testament. Attis, Adonis, and Osiris are in no sense historical characters. They are ideal embodiments of the decay and reanimation of natural life year by year. Even if the apostles knew of such myths there is no evidence that they suggested to them the idea of a resurrection of their Master. All the evidence shows that the last thing the disciples expected was such a resurrection. The change in their attitude came about suddenly. It was not a slow growth, and it claimed to be based on an alleged occurrence which it was within the power and in the interest of many to disprove had it been but a myth —the empty grave on the third day together with His subsequent appearings. This was their own explanation of the ethical and spiritual power which differentiates their belief from that of alleged pagan counterparts, and this is the only explanation that is adequate to the facts.

LITERATURE.—On the Mythological Theory see, further, **J. Orr,** *Resurrection of Jesus,* London, 1908, ch. ix. ; **T. J. Thorburn,** *Jesus the Christ: Historical or Mythical?,* Edinburgh, 1912 ; **R. J. Knowling,** *Testimony of St. Paul to Christ,* London, 1905, p. 282 ff.

3. *The Spiritual Significance Theory*

Another tendency which is dominant at the present time is that which lays emphasis on the spiritual worth or significance of the resurrection of Christ while surrendering or sitting loose to the belief in a bodily rising from the grave. A bodily Resurrection, so far from being of the essence of the Christian faith, is represented as a temporary excrescence which can be dropped without affecting it in any vital way.

This is a tendency associated especially with a certain section of the Ritschlian school of theologians and "connects itself naturally with the disposition in this school to seek the ground of faith in an immediate religious impression—in something verifiable on its own account—and to dissociate faith from doubtful questions of criticism and uncertainties of historical inquiry" (Orr, *Resurrection of Jesus,* p. 23 f.). "The basis of faith must be something fixed ; the results of historical study are continually changing (W. Herrmann, *Communion of the Christian with God,* Eng. tr.[2], London, 1906, p. 76). The certainty to which Christian faith holds fast is that "Christ lives," but this is a "judgment of value," or, as Herrmann prefers to call it, a "thought of faith" (*Glaubensgedanke*), a conviction based on the impression of religious worth produced by the earthly life of Jesus, and not affected by any view that may be held as to the historical Resurrection.   The belief in the Resurrection is thus not a belief based on historical evidence in regard to an event in the past, but a faith inference from a prior judgment of His person.

Foremost among representatives of this position stands Harnack, who has probably done more than any other to popularize the theory.   In his *Hist. of Dogma* (i. 85–87) he contends (1) that there is no satisfactory historical evidence of the actual bodily Resurrection.   "None of Christ's opponents saw him after his death. . . . The succession and number of the appearances can no longer be ascertained with certainty. . . . The disciples, and Paul, were conscious of having seen Christ not in the crucified earthly body, but in heavenly glory. . . . Even the empty grave on the third day can by no means be regarded as a certain historical fact, because it appears united in the accounts with manifest legendary features, and further because it is directly excluded by the way in which Paul has portrayed the resurrection in 1 Cor. xv."   But (2) Harnack goes further, and pours ridicule on the attempt to find such evidence.   He scouts the idea of faith being dependent on historical evidence at all.   Faith must be independent of evidence coming to us through the testimony of others.   "To believe in appearances which others have had is a frivolity which is always revenged by rising doubt."   But the faith which is thus independent of historical evidence is, it speedily appears, a faith which is indifferent to the question of the physical Resurrection. "Faith has by no means to do with the knowledge of the form in which Jesus lives, but only with the conviction that he is the living Lord." The faith in the Resurrection and the belief in the empty tomb are two different things. The historical question and the question of faith must clearly be distinguished here. In his later lectures on "What is Christianity?" Harnack gives expression to the same view in his famous distinction between what he calls the "Easter message" and the "Easter faith." "The Easter *message* tells us of that wonderful event in Joseph of Arimathæa's garden, which, however, no eye saw; it tells us of the empty grave into which a few women and disciples looked; of the appearance of the Lord in a transfigured form—so glorified that his own could not immediately recognise him; it soon begins to tell us, too, of what the risen one said and did." But "the Easter *faith* is the conviction that the crucified one gained a victory over death; that God is just and powerful; that he who is the first-born among many brethren still lives" (*What is Christianity?*[3], p. 163 f.). To found the Easter faith on the Easter message is to rest it on an "unstable foundation." "What he [Paul] and the disciples regarded as all-important was not the state in which the grave was found, but Christ's appearances. But who of us can maintain that a clear account of these appearances can be constructed out of the stories told by Paul and the evangelists; and if that be impossible, and there is no tradition of single events which is quite trustworthy, how is the Easter faith to be based on them? Either we must decide to rest our belief on a foundation unstable and always exposed to fresh doubts, or else we must abandon this foundation altogether, and with it the miraculous appeal to our senses" (p. 164 f.). It must have been, he thinks, even to the disciples themselves not so much the Easter message as the impression of His personality which was the ultimate foundation of the Easter faith that He was still alive. This impression of the personality of Jesus at least is a simple matter of fact which no historical criticism can in any way alter (*ib.*).

This position is open to objection on the following grounds :

(1) It is based on a view of the relation of faith and history—an attempt to make faith independent of historical evidence—which cannot be accepted. Mere historical evidence, indeed, is incompetent of itself to generate true Christian faith in the Resurrection. For this there is needed also an estimate of the moral and religious uniqueness of Jesus derived from the impression of His personality, which prepares the mind for the proper appreciation of the evidence. Only to those who have received this impression is the Resurrection truly credible. In this sense it is true to say that the belief in the Resurrection is a " value judgment" or " thought of faith"; and that "no appearances of the Lord could permanently have convinced them [the disciples] of his life, if they had not possessed in their hearts the impression of his Person" (*Hist. of Dogma*, i. 86 n.). But this is not to make faith independent of historical evidence. It may be and is involved in a proper estimate of His worth that "He could not be holden of death," which means not merely that " Jesus lives," as the Ritschlians put it, but that " He is risen from the dead." But, if all historical evidence for the fact were either wanting or

discredited at the bar of criticism, faith would be involved in insoluble contradiction. The Easter faith cannot dispense with the Easter message which is its historical attestation, an attestation which has to be judged by the principles of historical criticism.

(2) When we take the position to the test of the narratives its inadequacy is further established. Harnack holds that the distinction between the Easter faith and the Easter message is one already drawn in the New Testament. "The story of Thomas is told for the exclusive purpose of impressing upon us that we must hold the Easter faith even without the Easter message : ' Blessed are they that have not seen and yet have believed.' The disciples on the road to Emmaus were blamed for not believing in the resurrection even though the Easter message had not yet reached them. The Lord is a Spirit, says Paul ; and this carries with it the certainty of his resurrection " (*What is Christianity ?*[3], p. 163 f.). But the support thus found involves a misrepresentation of the facts. The words to Thomas (John xx. 29) are a rebuke to him for distrusting the testimony of his fellow-disciples and refusing to believe the Easter message without the personal verification of it by his own senses. The reproach to the two on the way to Emmaus (Luke xxiv. 25 f.) is directed against their hesitation to believe the story of the women, confirmed as this was by prophetic prediction, and the previous intimations of Jesus Himself. St. Paul's conviction that the Lord is the Spirit is the direct outcome of the appearing to him of the Risen Christ outside Damascus, which he reckons in the same category as the

earlier Appearings to the other apostles.   The stress
St. Paul lays on the Appearings as evidence of the
resurrection of Christ (1 Cor. xv. 5–8), combined with
his reference to the Burial, altogether forbids the attempt
to detach his Easter faith, or that of the early Christian
community, with which in these matters he knew himself to be at one, from the Easter message.   " It would
have conveyed no meaning to Paul or to any member of
the original Christian circle to say that it was the spirit
of Christ which rose into new life, or that He rose again
in the faith of His devoted followers, who could not bear
the thought that for Him death should end all " (Denney,
Jesus and the Gospel, p. 113).   The rising of which they
speak is relative to the grave and the burial.   They did
not need to be assured that His spirit survived death.
Not one of them doubted that.   What they did need to
be assured of, if their faith in Jesus was to be re-
established, was His victory over death and the grave,
and nothing but a bodily resurrection would have convinced them of that.

It may be, as A. E. Garvie suggests (*Studies in the
Inner Life of Jesus*, London, 1907, p. 439), " that Jesus
Himself would have esteemed the *Easter-faith*, the conviction that His life and work were of such infinite value
to God that He must prove the conqueror of death,
without the *Easter message*—the sensible evidences of
the reality of His resurrection—as much more precious
than this belief which rested on the signs of sense."
As during His earthly ministry He rated low the faith
that rested on His miracles (John iv. 48), so the belief
in His resurrection which needed sensible evidence might

be less satisfactory to Him, because showing less spiritual discernment of His worth, than a humble and confident trust in His word.   And for us to-day brought up within the Christian Church, the heirs of the past with the evidence of Christ's working through the centuries before us, belief in the Risen Lord may not depend so immediately or directly on the historical testimony of the Empty Grave and the Appearings.   But if one thing is made more plain and certain by the narratives than another it is that the disciples were quite incapable of the belief without the Easter message.   Deeply as He had stamped Himself upon them in His earthly intercourse, the disaster of His death paralyzed their faith in Him, and this was regained and reconstituted only through the Easter message of the Empty Grave and the subsequent Appearings.

But, it may be said, the Easter message, though thus needful, from the point of view of the early Christian community, to re-establish their faith and thus set the Church agoing—all the more so that for them as Jews a resurrection without an empty grave was unthinkable— is no longer necessary to the Christian faith, and may be dropped without affecting it in any vital way.   Essential to the first disciples, so essential that as a matter of history the Apostolic Church sprang from the conviction that the body of Jesus was not left in the grave, it is no longer essential to us to-day.   The Christian faith, it is urged, is not bound up with holding a particular view of the relation of the Glorified Christ to the body that was laid in Joseph's tomb.   Faith, it is said, is to be exercised in the Exalted Lord, and of this faith belief in a resurrection of the Body is no vital part.   This is the

13

position taken up in the latest outstanding illustration of
the attempt to conserve a spiritual Resurrection while
denying or minimizing the fact of a bodily resuscitation
—that of Sanday in his pamphlet *Bishop Gore's Challenge
to Criticism* (1914). Sanday is of opinion that we ought
to be satisfied with a heart-felt expression of the conviction that the Risen Lord as spirit still governs and
inspires His Church, while sitting loose to the question
of what became of His body. In regard to the resuscitation of the body of the Lord from the tomb, " the
accounts that have come down to us seem to be too conflicting and confused to prove this. But they do seem
to prove that in any case the detail is of less importance
than is supposed. Because, whatever it was, the body
which the disciples saw was not the natural human body
that was laid in the grave. . . . The central meaning of
the Resurrection is just that expressed in the vision of
the Apocalypse: ' I am the first and the last, and the
Living one ; and I was dead, and behold, I am alive
for evermore' (Rev. i. 18) " (p. 20). All else in the
apostolic representation is unessential for us to-day, and
can be spared. The bodily Resurrection is but a " sym-
bolical " representation of the essential fact, the result of
the world of ideas in which the first disciples moved.
Their world of ideas was one in which the resurrection
was conceived as a bodily resuscitation. Their " minds
were steeped in the Old Testament " and their " thoughts
naturally ran into the moulds which the Old Testament
supplied " (p. 24 f.), with its belief in " nature-miracles "
gathering round great personalities in a pre-scientific age
—a belief which " perpetuated itself in the New Testa-

ment" (p. 27). For the first disciples, therefore, the
"nature-miracle" of the bodily Resurrection "seemed
necessary to the completeness of the idea, but it is so no
longer." It "has done its work and can be spared. It
is like a lame man laying aside his crutches" (p. 28).

Sanday's position may be further elucidated by reference to a
sermon of his published some years previously in *Miracles* (London,
1911). "It was in Jewish circles that the belief in the Resurrection
first sprang up. . . . But among the Jews the characteristic form of
the belief in a life after death, or (as they expressed it) 'life from
the dead,' was the Pharisaic doctrine of a bodily resurrection. This
was the form of the belief which the first disciples had in their
minds, and which naturally and inevitably shaped and coloured all
their experiences. This was pre-eminently so with St. Paul, who
before his conversion had been a zealous Pharisee. . . . So it was in
the last resort this Pharisaic doctrine that was taken over by the
Christian Church, and that from the first dictated the form of the
Christian conception. It could not be otherwise. It was the one
alternative open to those who believed in life from the dead at all.
In that mould the belief of the first disciples was cast, and it has
remained dominant in the Church down to our own time" (p. 16 f.).
But it is characteristic of our time to attempt "to go behind this
form of the belief," to show how it arose naturally in certain
circumstances, and to distinguish between the question of its origin
and that of its permanent validity. "And I for one do not feel
that I can condemn those attempts. I do not think that we are
called upon to regard the precise form of the Pharisaic doctrine as
the last word on the subject. It is . . . only the relative expression or outward clothing of a Divine revelation. . . . It was through
the medium of minds possessed and dominated by these ideas, and,
indeed, practically not conscious of the existence of any other, that
the first announcement that Christ was alive and not dead was
given to the world" (p. 17 f.). But we have to distinguish between
"what the ancients themselves really thought" and "what we
moderns should think." Indeed this is "the main problem before
us at the present day" (p. 23).

The view of "nature-miracle" at the root of Sanday's
position will be examined in the following section, but

meanwhile two considerations may be urged in criticism of this depreciation of the bodily Resurrection :

(1) It is no doubt true that faith to-day is to be exercised directly in an Exalted and Glorified Lord, but our faith must ultimately rest on historical fact, and it is difficult to understand how Christian faith can ever be really indifferent or " agnostic " with regard to the facts about the empty tomb and the Risen Body which form so essential a part of the apostolic evidence.   To make the belief in the physical Resurrection of merely temporary significance—to set the Apostolic Church agoing—while now it may be cast aside as " no longer necessary," is to spurn the ladder by which we have risen to our Christian faith and to leave this faith " in the air."   It is difficult, if not impossible, to conceive how faith in an Exalted Lord could ever have been attained if the fact of the bodily resurrection of Jesus had not first been recognized. It is founded basally on the belief that the resurrection of Jesus was the actual raising in glory and power of that which was sown in dishonour and weakness ; and faith can never be indifferent to this its historical foundation.

(2) To sit loose to the bodily resurrection of Jesus is to do less than justice to the fullness of the apostolic representation of the essential constitutive significance of the Resurrection for the Christian faith (see above, p. 156 ff.). The rising of Jesus from the grave was for the Apostles at once the guarantee and the ground of the Christian's full redemption and immortality, body as well as spirit having its place in the renewed Kingdom of God, " who shall fashion anew the body of our humiliation that it may be conformed to the body of his glory " (Phil. iii. 21).

If the body of Jesus rotted away in the grave, then what guarantee have we that material forces are not after all supreme, and that Christ is indeed Lord over all, in nature as well as in grace, Lord of life and of death? The Resurrection-Body is indeed, as we have seen, not the same natural human body that was laid in the grave. It is this body so changed as to be described as a "spiritual" body, but this is very different from representing it as simply dropped and lost, abandoned to dissolution and decay. The plain question to be answered is, Was the Body of Jesus left lying in the tomb on the hillside of Jerusalem, or in some other tomb there to see corruption or was it not? If it was, what then? Let us suppose it to be firmly established that, instead of being raised, the body of Jesus was for some reason removed from the tomb in which it was first laid, and buried elsewhere, and that this or something like this is all the ground there is, beyond the pious imaginations of the disciples, for the belief that the body of Jesus was raised from the grave. On this supposition the apostolic doctrine of redemption becomes seriously attenuated, and our Christian faith turns out to be a very different thing from what it was for the early Church.

The view under criticism is really based not so much on a scientific examination of the historical evidence as on a dogmatic or philosophical attitude which, while seeking to preserve what is essential to Christian faith, would sacrifice the supernatural in the physical realm as being what Herrmann explicitly calls it, "a great hindrance to men to-day" (*Communion*[2], p. 80) in the way of accepting Christianity. That this is so is recognized with characteristic frankness by Sanday in the pamphlet referred to.   It is professedly because he finds the evidence on behalf of the bodily Resurrection unsatisfactory that he ranges himself with the "modernists" in doubting the fact.   But this denial or minimizing of the bodily Resurrection is made, he recognizes, in an apologetic interest, viz. for the sake of commending Christianity to the "modern mind" by removing what he calls "the greatest of all stumbling-blocks" in the way of its acceptance, the admission of miracle in the physical realm.   "I know," he says, "that the suggestions I have made will come with a shock to the great mass of Christians; but in the end I believe that they will be thankfully welcomed.   What they would mean is that the greatest of all stumbling-blocks to the modern mind is removed, and that the beautiful regularity that we see around us now has been, and will be, the law of the Divine action from the beginning to the end of time" (*Bishop Gore's Challenge*, p. 30).   The ground of this repugnance to the recognition of the physical supernatural or "nature-miracle" will be considered in the following section.

LITERATURE.—On the Spiritual-Significance Theory see **J. H. Skrine,** *Miracle and History,* London, 1912; **J. Orr,** *The Christian View of God and the World,* Edinburgh, 1893, lect. vi. note C (p. 512 ff.); **D. W. Forrest,** *Christ of History and of Experience*[7], do., 1914, p. 158 ff.; **B. Lucas,** *Fifth Gospel,* London, 1907, p. 160; **H. Hensley Henson,** *Hibbert Journal,* ii. 476.

4. *The "Supernatural-without-Miracle" Theory*

The real *motif* of all theories which attempt to explain the apostolic belief in the Resurrection without accepting the full apostolic representation of the fact is the repugnance to the admission of the supernatural in any specific or unique sense in the physical realm. This is the presupposition or *præjudicium* lying behind and determining the attitude of modern thought to the evidence; so that the fundamental apologetic problem to-day in connexion with the Resurrection is, as it has been in all ages, the problem of the supernatural. The latest evidence of this is the attitude of Sanday to the bodily Resurrection as definitely elicited by his controversy with Gore. His "entire and strong belief in the central reality of the . . . Supernatural Resurrection" Sanday affirms (*Bishop Gore's Challenge to Criticism*, p. 28); but he claims that this need not involve the admission of the "nature-miracle" of the resuscitation of the Body from the tomb. Sanday adopts the old distinction between *contra naturam* and *supra naturam* miracles. The latter, the "healing-miracles" of the Gospels, "were abundantly accounted for by the presence in the world of a unique Personality, and by that wave of new spiritual force which flowed from it in ever-increasing volume. They involved no real breach in the order of nature" (p. 24). The "nature-miracles" of the Gospels, however, with the bodily resurrection of Jesus as the supreme instance, are represented as not merely thus *supra naturam* but as *contra naturam*, involving a "definite reversal of the natural physical order" (p. 23). The conception of "nature-miracles" "took its rise in the region of the Old Testament," through the influence of myths or legends gathering round great personalities in a pre-scientific age, and "perpetuated itself in the New

Testament" (p. 27).   But the admission of such miracles is contrary to the postulate of modern science, the uniformity of nature, "the beautiful regularity that we see around us . . . the law of the Divine action from the beginning to the end of time" (p. 30), and must be dropped.   So the watchword of much current Christian apologetic in its attempt to recommend Christianity to the "modern mind" is "the supernatural without miracles."   This is the point of view represented in an extreme form by J. M. Thompson's *Miracles in the New Testament* (London, 1911).

At the root of this modern repugnance to the supernatural in the physical region lies the conception of miracle as a "violation of natural law," or "a breach in the order of nature."   This is the view of miracle which, *e.g.*, controls Schmiedel's negative criticism.   "By miracle we here throughout understand an occurrence that unquestionably is against natural law" (*Encycl. Bibl.* iv. 4040).   This is the view which already underlay Hume's famous argument in his essay "On Miracles" (*Essays, Moral, Political and Literary*, 2 vols., ed. London, 1907) as to the insufficiency of evidence for the alleged Gospel miracles in face of our experience of the regularity of nature, and of the notorious fallibility of human testimony to extraordinary events.   "A miracle is a violation of the laws of nature; and as a firm and unalterable experience has established these laws, the proof against a miracle, from the very nature of the fact, is as entire as any argument from experience can possibly be imagined" (ii. 93).   He takes the Resurrection as his typical example.   "It is no miracle that a man . . . should die

on a sudden : because such a kind of death . . . has yet
been frequently observed to happen.   But it is a miracle,
that a dead man should come to life ; because that has
never been observed, in any age or country " (*ib.*).
Briefly, it is contrary to experience that a miracle should
be true, but not contrary to experience that human
testimony should be false (cf. ii. 105).   While the
" healing-miracles " of the Gospel, or most of them, may
be scientifically explicable in accordance with laws
recognized by modern science (what M. Arnold called
" moral therapeutics "), the " nature-miracles," with the
bodily Resurrection as the supreme instance, are ruled out
as violations of natural law.

This objection to nature-miracles, however, goes back
to a view of nature and natural law which, as the off-
spring of a mechanical view of the world, is now obsolete,
yet which continues to influence thought in subtle ways.
If nature be regarded as a closed mechanical system
owing its origin, it may be, to the creative power and
wisdom of the Divine, but now a self-sufficient, self-
running order bound together by iron bonds of natural
law, then what we call " miracle " can be conceived only
as an intervention from without, an inroad or intrusion
into an ordered and complete mechanical whole.   But if
nature, as a more adequate philosophy is now teaching
us, and as science itself is increasingly recognizing, is no
such closed mechanical system shut in upon itself, but
alive, moving, a growing organism, a process of creative
evolution ; if its laws are not ultimate realities or entities
which bind the universe into a changeless mechanism of
material forces, but simply modes of the Divine activity,

forms of God's self-expression—then a very different conception of miracle presents itself. The distinction between "natural" and "supernatural" becomes a distinction between lower and higher forms of Divine activity. What is called the "natural order" is God's basal method of working in the world, the indispensable condition of all stable rational experience. What are called the "laws of nature" are the general laws of sequence based on past observation and experience of the Divine working on this basal level—" a convenient short-hand method of summing up our existing knowledge" —whereby we can say that if the same conditions are fulfilled the same results will follow. In this sense nature is "uniform" or "regular." If the conditions are changed, however, and new forces are introduced whereby a new level of Divine working is brought about, the ordinary laws of nature are not violated or contradicted but transcended, their action is controlled or modified for higher ends. Standing at the lower level and without experience of the higher, the new experiences may seem to contradict what is natural at that level, to be in that sense *contra naturam*, while really, as St. Augustine long ago pointed out, being only "contrary to nature so far as yet known" ("non contra naturam, sed contra quam est nota natura" [*de Civ. Dei*, xxi. 8]). From the point of view of the physical order the phenomena of organic nature and still more of self-conscious personality will appear as if they contradicted the laws of that order. They would be contradictory only if these laws were assumed to be final and ultimate instead of being part of a larger whole, means to ends beyond themselves. (This point is suggestively dealt with by D. S. Cairns in his little book *The Reasonableness of the Christian Faith*, London, 1918, pp. 90 ff. and 154 ff.)

Apply this to the nature-miracles of Jesus, and in particular to His bodily resurrection.   If we regard Jesus of Nazareth as one whose life moved wholly on the plane of our ordinary human experience, the *contra naturam* argument might be urged with plausibility. But in Jesus, as the narratives present Him, we have a new phenomenon in human history, unique in His character, person, and work.   He stood in the midst of a sinful world, the alone sinless One, living in perfect communion with God, and claiming a unique relation to God and man—a claim which He substantiated in the experience of those who submitted themselves to Him, making them veritably " new creations."   This is a miracle in the moral and spiritual sphere as wonderful as any alleged miracle in the physical.   It is a new departure in human history—in this sense " contrary to experience "—so that we cannot criticize Him by the light of any canons drawn from our past experience of ordinary humanity.   In the case of such a new phenomenon we should antecedently expect that He would manifest Himself in new and unfamiliar ways. " As with the appearance of man there were introduced new powers and properties unimaginable from the animal point of view and therefore from that point of view seemingly supernatural—so with the appearance of the Christ we ought to expect new powers and properties unimaginable from the human point of view and therefore to us seemingly supernatural, *i.e. above our nature*" (J. le

Conte, *Evolution in Relation to Religious Thought*, London, 1888, p. 362).

Human personality is a unity in which spiritual and material are organically connected and mutually dependent, the spirit moulding the body and the body in turn influencing the spirit. Sin, accordingly, is a fact which though primarily moral and spiritual—a matter of the will—yet extends to and includes the physical as well, moral and physical mingling with and reacting on each other till the entire resultant may be spoken of as " this body of death " (Rom. vii. 24)—" a complex whole in which it is impossible to disentangle the spiritual element from the diseased conditions and perverted functions of organ and tissue, which personal and ancestral sins have brought about " (Illingworth, *Divine Immanence*, p. 92). In like manner sinlessness is a fact which, though primarily moral and spiritual, concerns the physical as well, a sinless soul carrying with it as its correlative an unstained body. It may be " contrary to experience," as Hume says, that a human body should rise from the dead; it is contrary to our experience, that is to say, of ordinary human bodies, the bodies of sinful men. But in the case of a sinless personality like that of Jesus we have a fact so transcending ordinary experience that no amount of evidence drawn from such experience can warrant us in laying down beforehand how nature will react on such an one. It may be as normal for a sinless man to rise from the dead as it is for the bodies of sinful men to remain in the grave. At all events our modern scientific knowledge of the mutual interdependence of spirit and body makes it *a priori*

probable that one who like Jesus was not holden of sin
should also not be holden of death.   Without this the
manifestation of His triumph over sin would be incomplete.   But more than this.   Jesus claimed not only
to be sinless Himself but to have come into the world
to destroy the dominion of sin in others.   He stood over
against men the alone sinless One claiming to have power
to forgive and to redeem, and, in manifestation of His
power to rectify the whole disorder caused by sin and
restore the entire personality of man, body as well as
soul, to God's plan for it, He performed works of healing
on the body.   His healing of the one He connected with
His forgiving of the other as parts of the same redemptive work.   Of this redemptive Lordship, His own
bodily resurrection was at once the consummating
manifestation and the final guarantee; so that being
such an One as He was and proved Himself to be *per
ejus beneficia* "it was not possible that he should be
holden of death" (Acts ii. 24).

It is in the light of these considerations that the
physical Resurrection becomes credible, and even antecedently probable.   It is not an isolated abnormal
incident in an otherwise normal career.   "If the Resurrection were alleged to have occurred abruptly in the
middle of a series of events which passed on slowly to
their consummation unaffected by its interruption . . .
then we might have paused in doubt before so stupendous
a miracle, and pleaded the uniformity of nature against
the claims of such an event upon our belief" (Westcott,
Gospel of the Resurrection, p. 105).   But the Resurrection
is the resurrection of Jesus, and, as such, an event at

once with unique antecedents and unique consequents.
Its context on either side is miraculous. It is the
culmination of a unique human life, a life which was a
moral miracle constituting a break in human experience,
and making such a physical miracle as the Resurrection
altogether natural and congruous; a life too which was
represented as the consummation of God's purposes in
all previous human history—for this is the essential
meaning of the appeal to prophecy made by the apostles.
Then there are the unique consequents of the fact—and
the nature of a cause becomes apparent only in the
effect—the rise of the Christian Church as a new and
ever-increasing power in history constituted in the
continuous miracle of Christian history and experience.
It is when we consider the Resurrection thus in its
context that we see the naturalness and congruousness
of the fact. As the consummation of the Incarnation
and the means of realizing its purposes, the Resurrection
is at once an end and a new beginning. "To this fact
all former history converges as to a certain goal; from
this fact all subsequent history flows as from its life-
giving spring" (*ib.* p. 104). And so, taking all the
evidence together—evidence converging and cumulative—
it is not too much to say with Westcott that "there is
no single historic incident better or more variously
supported than the resurrection of Christ" (*ib.* p. 137).

LITERATURE.—On the Resurrection and the supernatural see **B. F.
Westcott**, *Gospel of the Resurrection*[6], London, 1888, pp. 15-54; **J. O. F.
Murray**, "The Spiritual and Historical Evidence for Miracles," in
Cambridge Theological Essays, ed. H. B. Swete, do., 1905, p. 311 ff.;
M. Dods, *The Supernatural in Christianity*[2] (in reply to Pfleiderer),
Edinburgh, 1894; **J. R. Illingworth**, *Divine Immanence*, London,
1898, *The Gospel Miracles*, do., 1915 (esp. ch. ii.); **A. C. Headlam**,

The Miracles of the New Testament, do., 1914 ; **A. J. Balfour**, *Theism and Humanism*, do., 1915 ; **H. Scott Holland**, in *Christian Commonwealth*, June 1914 (criticism of Sanday) ; **J. F. Bethune-Baker**, *The Miracle of Christianity*, London, 1914 ; **F. H. Chase**, *Belief and Creed*, do., 1918 ; **C. W. Emmet**, *Conscience, Creeds and Critics*, do., 1918.

General Literature Note

The chief relevant literature on the various aspects of the subject has been indicated in the body of the article. On the whole subject the older works of **B. F. Westcott**, *The Gospel of the Resurrection*[1], London, 1865, *The Revelation of the Risen Lord*,[2] do., 1882, **W. Milligan**, *The Resurrection of our Lord*, do., 1881, *Ascension and Heavenly Priesthood of our Lord*, do., 1892, and **S. D. F. Salmond**, *The Christian Doctrine of Immortality*, Edinburgh, 1895, are not yet superseded. Among more recent works covering the whole field the more important are **A. Meyer**, *Die Auferstehung Christi*, Freiburg i. B., 1905 ; **L. Ihmels**, *Die Auferstehung Jesu Christi*, Leipzig, 1906 ; **J. Orr**, *The Resurrection of Jesus*, London, 1908 ; **C. H. Robinson**, *Studies in the Resurrection of Christ*, do., 1909 ; **W. J. Sparrow Simpson**, *Our Lord's Resurrection*, do., 1905, *The Resurrection and Modern Thought*, do., 1911. Cf. **E. R. Bernard**, art. "Resurrection," *Hastings' Dict. of Bible*, iv. 231–236 ; **W. J. Sparrow Simpson**, art. "Resurrection of Christ," *Hastings' Dict. of Christ and Gospels*, ii. 505–514.

INDEX

PRINTED BY
MORRISON AND GIBB LIMITED
EDINBURGH